W9-CEE-209

A LIFE OF
JESUS
THE CHRIST

FROM
COSMIC ORIGINS
TO THE SECOND
COMING

RICHARD HENRY DRUMMOND, PH.D.

St. Martin's Paperbacks

NOTE: If you purchased this book without a cover you should be aware that this book is stolen property. It was reported as "unsold and destroyed" to the publisher, and neither the author nor the publisher has received any payment for this "stripped book."

All Scripture quotations, unless otherwise noted, are from the *Revised Standard Version of the Bible*, Old Testament Section, Copyright 1952; New Testament Section, First Edition, Copyright 1946; Second Edition © 1971 by Division of Christian Education of the National Council of Churches of Christ in the United States of America.

A LIFE OF JESUS THE CHRIST: FROM COSMIC ORIGINS TO THE SECOND COMING

Copyright © 1989 by Richard Henry Drummond.

Cover photograph by Photonica.

All rights reserved. No part of this book may be used or reproduced in any manner whatsoever without written permission except in the case of brief quotations embodied in critical articles or reviews. For information address St. Martin's Press, 175 Fifth Avenue, New York, N.Y. 10010.

Library of Congress Catalog Card Number: 89-45239

ISBN: 0-312-96057-3

Printed in the United States of America

Harper & Row trade paperback edition published in 1989
St. Martin's Paperbacks edition/December 1996

10 9 8 7 6 5 4 3 2 1

WHO WAS EDGAR CAYCE?

Edgar Cayce was born in 1877 in Hopkinsville, Kentucky and lived sixty-seven years that were sometimes painfully eventful, but tremendously enlightening. He had developed a gift in former lifetimes which gave him the capacity in this life to enter a state of altered consciousness. He was able to be in touch with the akashic records and the information in what he called the Universal Consciousness.

In his state of altered consciousness, Cayce would respond to questions and often would give special dissertations on a variety of subjects. Two thirds of his nearly 15,000 readings had to do with healing of the human body. He is well-known, too, for his predictions on earth changes and his readings on reincarnation, dreams, soul development, Christ consciousness, astrology, Atlantis, ancient Egypt, and emotional development. Cayce's readings evidenced a very close relationship with Jesus and his teachings, and it is not surprising that he advised hundreds who sought his counsel to take Jesus as their pattern for living in these troublesome times.

Cayce could also contact the unconscious mind of individuals far distant from where he was giving a reading, and could describe not only their past lives, but also the state of the inquirer's physiological functioning and what needed to be done to return that individual to full health.

Cayce's legacy for the world can be found not only in the hearts and minds of millions of individuals whose lives he has changed, but also at the Association for Research and Enlightenment (A.R.E.) Library in Virginia Beach, VA, which houses the Cayce Readings.

Edgar called his work the work of the Christ, and anyone who studies these readings to any depth will most likely agree.

William A. McGarey, M.D.

BOOKS IN THE EDGAR CAYCE SERIES
FROM ST. MARTIN'S PAPERBACKS

KEYS TO HEALTH by Eric Mein, M.D.

REINCARNATION: CLAIMING YOUR PAST, CREATING
   YOUR FUTURE by Lynn Elwell Sparrow

DREAMS: TONIGHT'S ANSWERS FOR TOMORROW'S
   QUESTIONS by Mark Thurston

AWAKENING YOUR PSYCHIC POWERS by Henry Reed

HEALING MIRACLES: USING YOUR BODY ENERGIES FOR
   SPIRITUAL AND PHYSICAL HEALTH by William A.
   McGarey, M.D.

A LIFE OF JESUS THE CHRIST: FROM COSMIC ORIGINS TO
   THE SECOND COMING by Richard Henry Drummond

COMING SOON:

MYSTERIES OF ATLANTIS REVISITED by Edgar Evans
   Cayce, Gail Cayce Schwartzer, and Douglas G.
   Richards

GROWING THROUGH PERSONAL CRISIS by Harmon
   Hartzell Bro with June Avis Bro

SOUL-PURPOSE: DISCOVERING AND FULFILLING YOUR
   DESTINY by Mark Thurston

MILES TO GO: THE SPIRITUAL QUEST OF AGING by
   Richard Peterson

CONTENTS

FOREWORD

IT IS A time in the earth when people everywhere seek to know more of the mysteries of the mind, the soul," said my grandfather, Edgar Cayce, from an unconscious trance from which he demonstrated a remarkable gift for clairvoyance.

His words are prophetic even today, as more and more Americans in these unsettled times are turning to psychic explanations for daily events. For example, according to a national survey by the National Opinion Research Council nearly half of American adults today believe they have been in contact with someone who has died, a figure twice that of ten years ago. Two-thirds of all adults say they have had an ESP experience; ten years ago that figure was only one-half.

Every culture throughout history has made note of its own members' gifted powers beyond the five senses. These rare individuals held special interest because they seemed able to provide solutions to life's pressing problems. And America in the twentieth century is no exception.

Edgar Cayce was perhaps the most famous and most carefully documented psychic of our time. He began to use his unusual abilities when he was a young man, and from then on for over forty years he would, usually twice a day, lie on a couch, go into a sleeplike state, and respond to questions. Over 14,000 of these discourses, called readings, were carefully transcribed by his secretary and preserved by the Edgar

Cayce Foundation in Virginia Beach, Virginia. These psychic readings continue to provide inspiration, insight, and physical help to tens of thousands of people.

Having only an eighth-grade education, Edgar Cayce lived a plain, simple life by the world's standards. As early as childhood in Hopkinsville, Kentucky, however, he sensed that he had psychic ability. While alone he had a vision of a woman who told him he would have unusual abilities to help people. Other times he related experiences of "seeing" dead relatives. Once, while struggling with school lessons, he slept on his spelling book and awakened knowing the entire contents of the book.

As a young man he experimented with hypnosis to treat his own recurring throat problem that caused him to lose his speech. He discovered that under hypnosis he could diagnose and describe treatments for the physical ailments of others, often without knowing or seeing the person with the ailment. People began to ask him other sorts of questions and he found himself able to answer these as well.

In 1910 the *New York Times* published a two-page story with pictures about Edgar Cayce's psychic ability as described by a young physician, Wesley Ketchum, to a clinical research society in Boston. From that time on people from all over the country with every conceivable question sought his help.

In addition to his unusual talents, Cayce was a deeply religious man who taught Sunday School all of his adult life and read the entire Bible once for every year that he lived. He always tried to attune himself to God's will by studying the Scriptures and maintaining a rich prayer life, as well as by trying to be of service to those who came seeking help. He used his talents only for helpful purposes. Cayce's simplicity and humility and his commitment to doing good in the world continue to attract people to the story of his life and work and to the far-reaching information he gave.

In this series we hope to provide the reader with insights in the search for understanding and meaning in life. Each book in the series explores its subject from the viewpoint of the Edgar Cayce readings and compares perspectives of other metaphysical literature and of current scientific thought. The interested reader needs no prior knowledge of the Edgar Cayce information. When one of the Edgar Cayce readings is quoted, the identifying number of that reading is included for those who may wish to read the full text. Each volume contains suggestions for further study.

This book, *A Life of Jesus the Christ* by Richard Henry Drummond, Ph.D., integrates information from the Edgar Cayce readings on the life of Jesus with information from the Bible in order to present a much more insightful portrayal than is found in most accounts. As a theologian, seminary professor, and Christian missionary, Dr. Drummond has devoted his life to studying and teaching the ministry of Jesus. In recent years, as a visiting scholar at Atlantic University, he conducted the research for this book, with the result that he writes as a leading Christian scholar who is superbly qualified to present this unique perspective from the Edgar Cayce readings on the life and ministry of Jesus Christ.

Charles Thomas Cayce

PREFACE

WHY A BOOK of this kind? There are not a few works available in English on the life and teaching of Jesus, some of them combining careful scholarship with readability and popular appeal: the German scholar Günther Bornkamm's *Jesus of Nazareth*; the Dutch theologian Edward Schillebeeckx's *Jesus: An Experiment in Chirstology*; or the distinguished Japanese Catholic novelist Shusaku Endo's *A Life of Jesus*. Modern historical-critical study of the Bible now has a history of more than two hundred years, perhaps beginning with the German scholar J. A. Bengel in the early eighteenth century. What more is needed?

Enormous time and effort have been expended over these past centuries in academically responsible biblical studies. They have been aided increasingly by modern archaeological excavations and the discovery of both ancient texts and innumerable artifacts. The so-called assured results of such scholarship, however, are relatively few, although these are not to be discounted, especially with reference to establishment of a reliable Hebrew/Aramaic and Greek text of the Bible.

Recent focus has been on "redaction criticism," a scholarly method whose primary concern is to identify the theological stance and motivation of the authors of particular books of the Bible. Of the several methodologies of biblical study developed, especially in the twentieth century, this has probably been the most successful. One should note also the earnest call to awareness of the public-political responsibility of biblical scholarship by Elizabeth Schussler Fiorenza in her presidential address to the Society of Biblical Literature in 1987.

Yet we can surely speak of a kind of malaise in biblical studies with reference to deeper issues of truth, especially religious or cosmic truth. In fact the focus of most recent biblical studies on issues of historical context and background, on questions of literary form, on the authorship and date of particular books or portions of books of the Bible, seems at times to suggest a quiet despair with reference to more final issues of truth.

A wide separation has emerged—perhaps wider than many realize—between the views, in their manifold variety, of academically oriented biblical scholars and those of others, even when the latter are well educated in the larger cultural sense. One reason for this separation has been the emergence of views of extreme skepticism among some academic biblical scholars, especially in Germany. For instance, Rudolf Bultmann came to the conclusion that we cannot be truly certain about one single word or teaching of Jesus in the New Testament. All we can know for sure, he said, is that Jesus of Nazareth lived and died. Bultmann's pietistic Lutheran faith in the risen Christ seemed somehow removed in its origins from the conclusions he himself drew from biblical scholarship. Somewhat on the other side, the German scholar Joachim Jeremias spent much of his life trying to ascertain and establish the *ipissima verba* (actual words) of Jesus within the scriptural records. He achieved some success, to be sure, but he often worked against very great odds in the larger academic community, especially in his own country.

One result of the above has been to encourage the rise of conservatism, political as well as religious, all across the world over the past fifteen to twenty years. In some circles this development has taken the form of various kinds of fundamentalism—at times strident, virulent, intellectually mind-less—visible in historically Islamic as well as Christian lands. In Christian context this development has led, admit-tedly as a distinctly minority phenomenon, to a reemergence of the concept-doctrine of biblical inerrancy and a total re-jection of both the methodology and results of modern his-torical-critical biblical scholarship. Many Christians and Jews, and evidently some Muslims as well, find themselves almost at a loss in the tug-of-war between these two ex-tremes, hoping somehow to find a golden mean closer to the middle.

The fact may be astonishing to some, but it is a fact that the clairvoyantly derived materials of Edgar Cayce, or of Rudolf Steiner—who have been called the two greatest clair-voyants of the Western world in the twentieth century—do furnish such a middle ground, especially with reference to the great or major themes of biblical faith. Indeed, if one were to place these materials within the spectrum of contem-porary biblical studies and theology, one would probably have to say that they are somewhat to the right of center.

There is a place, therefore, for a book of this kind, which makes use of materials derived from the methodology of clairvoyant perception as one of its sources in a comparative study. Clairvoyance here is treated as one potentially legiti-mate element in a process of interdisciplinary studies, whereby the participants continue to make use of traditional academic disciplines—in this instance of biblical content, use of linguistics in the widest sense of the term, use of textual criticism, historical and anthropological studies, sociology, psychology, and continuing rapport with archeological dis-coveries in the Middle East and elsewhere—in a constant process of comparison, of checks and balances. This process, however, is not only academic. It includes continuing partic-ipation in the life of historic churches and synagogues, in their worship, in their fellowship and their service of others.

Like Edgar Cayce in his own lifetime (1877–1945), I would not presume to enter into a task of this kind without having also participated in a disciplined religious life of many years duration. No work of this kind, whether of Edgar Cayce or of the present author, can be properly evaluated without also weighing the personal character of the individuals involved.

I use the term clairvoyance here in the broad sense of including intuition or insight, daydreaming, even hunches or other modes of what we now call altered states of consciousness. I use the word as also comprising dreams, visions and the "still small voice," the methods identified in the Bible as the primary means by which biblical personages received what they believed to be divine inspiration. I am speaking specifically of direct perception of what Rudolf Steiner preferred to call "supersensible realities" by means of human faculties beyond the five physical senses.

The entire history of humanity, in every part of the world, shows us—and continues to show us—examples of this kind of perception, or reception. The success of the activity has clearly varied, evidently depending in no small measure upon the personal character of the individuals involved in the process and the nature as well as extent to which they participate in the comparisons and other disciplines cited above. But that the methodology is potentially valid is at least suggested by Sir James Jeans, the distinguished British astronomer active in the earlier half of this century. Jeans said that any real extension of human knowledge, even in the realm of natural science, "waits upon the evolution or development of further senses of perception."

Creative work in many fields—not only in religion or in the arts and literature, but also in business and government, and indeed in natural science as well—owes its origin in many cases to insights operating beyond the levels of ordinary rational processes of thought. One of the best-known examples of creative dreaming in the composition of great literature is Samuel Taylor Coleridge's poem "Kubla Khan." Coleridge is said to have perceived the bulk of it, indeed composed it himself, during sleep of an hour or more's duration late one day in the year 1797. The Hungarian biochemist Albert Szent-Györgyi, who was awarded the 1937 Nobel prize for medicine and physiology and emigrated to the United States in 1947, said, "My work is not finished when I leave my workbench in the afternoon. I go on thinking about my problems all the time, and my brain must continue to think about them when I sleep, because I wake up, sometimes in the middle of the night, with answers to questions that have been puzzling me."

On March 1, 1869, the young Russian scientist Dmitri Mendeleyev perceived in a state of altered consciousness akin to daydreaming what became the celebrated periodic table of elements. By a similar methodology the German chemist F. A. Kekulé von Stradonitz in 1865 was able to perceive the atomic structure of a whole group of cyclic or ring compounds in organic chemistry, particularly the benzene ring. With reference to biblical insight we may recall the ability of the seventeenth-century British poet Thomas Traherne to perceive inwardly in vivid detail many events of biblical history.

These men were all specialists in their fields, and so were able to understand and evaluate the significance of what they had perceived by transnormal means. They went on to test their perceptions by the long and arduous processes of the ordinary methods of natural science, the social sciences—or biblical studies. They performed experiments, made mathematical calculations, carried on linguistic, historical, and other appropriate studies. Above all, they submitted their perceptions and the results of their studies to colleagues and friends for verification and possible correction or supplementation. The consequences of all human perception are properly tested as much by their application to everyday human experience, as by their inner coherence and consistency with facts known by a variety of methodologies. You who read this book are invited to test its contents by these and any other means that you are able to bring to bear.

You may be aware of my book *Unto the Churches*, written

just over ten years ago and now in its third printing. In this book I treated material similar to that which is found in the present volume. I hasten to say, however, that the present work is more than a revision. It is the result of a complete rewriting. Indeed every sentence has been rewritten, and much new material has been added.

I have grown personally as well as academically over these years. Academically I have concentrated on biblical studies in both research and teaching to a degree perhaps beyond that of any other period of my professional life. I have continued regularly to teach courses in this field, especially in New Testament studies and in the early church fathers, at the University of Dubuque Theological Seminary, at Tokyo Union Theological Seminary, at Meiji Gakuin University in Tokyo, Japan, and at Atlantic University in Virginia Beach, Virginia. I have lectured in these areas in Korea, Germany, and Switzerland. The result, I believe, is a work of careful scholarship, as well as of personal insight, wrought toward the end of a long and happy life of Christian service.

I wish especially to thank my wife Pearl Estella Drummond for her work in proofreading and even more for the challenges to critical assessment that she has given me. I wish also sincerely to thank my sister Eleanor E. Drummond-Meyer for her careful work in proofreading. Mr. A. Robert Smith, editor of the magazine *Venture Inward*, deserves my deep gratitude for his careful and helpful work of basic editing of the manuscript. I hereby also express my warm thanks to Dr. Charles Thomas Cayce, president of the Association for Research and Enlightenment, for his consistent encouragement and support in the entire process of writing and publication. My sincere thanks are also due Dr. James C. Windsor, president of Atlantic University, for his help in the original inception of this book and for his continued encouragement in the writing. I want to thank Janie West for her careful typing and conscientious structuring of the whole process of putting the manuscript on computer.

I wish also to thank most warmly the kind friends and

colleagues who read my manuscript and wrote prepublication comments. These are Dr. William D. Bray, emeritus professor of New Testament, Kwansei Gakuin University, Nishinomiya, Japan; Dr. Harmon Hartzell Bro, psychotherapist and theologian, formerly dean, Drake University Divinity School; the Reverend Dr. John Foss, senior minister, Bella Vista Community Church, Bella Vista, Arkansas; Dr. Bengt Hoffman, emeritus professor of historical theology, Lutheran Theological Seminary, Gettysburg, Pennsylvania; Dr. Geddes MacGregor, emeritus distinguished professor of philosophy, University of Southern California; the Reverend Dr. Douglas C. Runnels, senior minister, Parkridge Community Church, Parkridge, Illinois; Dr. C. Howard Wallace, professor of Old Testament literature and interpretation, University of Dubuque Theological Seminary, Dubuque, Iowa.

I am greatly in debt to our older son, the Reverend Donald Craig Drummond, who has kindly used his knowledge and expertise to prepare the index of this book.

INTRODUCTION

THE READINGS OF Edgar Cayce are the stenographically transcribed verbatim records of his clairvoyant activity. They consist of his responses to questions asked of him and suggestions made after he had put himself into an altered state of consciousness through selfhypnosis. Harmon Hartzell Bro has suggested that this altered state can appropriately be called an extension of Cayce's prayer life. He unfailingly entered this state only after personally praying for divine protection and guidance. The process functioned also in the most direct relationship with his daily conscious life. Cayce found that this activity worked best when he remained true to the highest ethical and religious standards of his conscious life.

The sources he drew upon were sometimes referred to in the readings as "universal." The key instrument was the subconscious mind of Edgar Cayce himself, able upon suggestion to communicate verbally through his natural voice its own knowledge, and, even more significantly, knowledge of the subconscious minds of others, from what Cayce called "soul memory." Cayce's questioning subconscious mind also sought out more distinctly universal sources of information called Akashic Records, purportedly written upon "the skein of time and space." What Harmon Bro has termed "some kind of swift intelligence" also seemed to preside over the process and to enable Cayce's subconscious to move through space, through realms of present knowledge, through history and beyond, giving medical, scientific, political, economic, moral, and religio-theological data of macrocosmic as well as microcosmic scope. Some of the material, by far the smaller part, was predictive—predictive, however, in the sense of Old Testament prophecy. That is, the predictions were not of absolutely predetermined events. In the case of warnings they were statements of open-ended trends that were expected to develop in such and such a way unless those concerned changed their minds and ways. If the persons changed, the developments of events could change. Other predictions were very positive and hopeful. Edgar Cayce, however, never claimed infallibility for himself, either for that expressed in the readings or for the products of his conscious mind.

The authenticity of these materials—that is, the truth of the content of the readings—needs therefore to be tested in the same way that other statements of fact or larger truth are tested. That is, the materials must be tested in terms of their own inner coherence and consistency and of their conformity to facts and truth of the same genre but already known, tested, and found—by some measure of consensus among responsible specialists—to be worthy of public consideration.

Not only scientific and historical truth, but also truth in the realm of philosophy and religion, is normally sought by this method of reciprocal comparison and testing. We may recall that Jesus himself is recorded as asking his hearers to test the authenticity of religious teachers through their fruits in life (Matt. 7:20).

Gautama the Buddha is also said to have offered a similar criterion in answer to a question as to how to distinguish between true and false religious teachers. His reply was in effect that people should judge for themselves, and their standard of judgment should be whether the teaching under consideration "when performed and undertaken" leads to moral loss and sorrow or the reverse, to the ethical degeneration of human beings or to their moral and spiritual development. The criterion for the authenticity of religious teachings for the Buddha was thus the ethical quality of the content of the teachings and their fruits in life. Presumably the religious authenticity of the teachers was also to be evaluated by the same standard. For most people, however, especially in the academic community, a quest for historical facts and cosmic truth through clairvoyant perception is a new way of investigating either history or theology. And as the Japanese sociologist of religion Minoru Kasai has put it, a new epistemology is needed for this new—for most—methodology. I contend, however, that a study of the knowledge gained through this mode of clairvoyant perception is very much worth the attempt in the case of certain notable persons in human history. I believe also that the validity of such knowledge can be reliably ascertained by the very same tests that are applied to data of comparable content obtained by other means. In this research piece on Jesus the Christ we shall endeavor therefore to correlate, and thereby test, the pertinent materials on Jesus given in the Edgar Cayce readings with the results of current academic scholarship. Above all, we shall try with especial care to compare them with the witness of the Bible itself.

THE HISTORICAL BASIS OF CLAIRVOYANT INVESTIGATION

From the standpoint of twentieth-century depth psychology, clairvoyant investigation may be considered an activity of the human unconscious and the resultant material a series of imaginary stories. But therapists who work with the unconscious often speak of its wisdom and note that what may be denoted as an imaginary story can in some cases solve a patient's primary problem. The great psychologist Carl Gustav Jung, in *Memories, Dreams, Reflections*, did not hesitate to identify what he had long believed to be the cosmic or religious referents in the activity of the human unconscious.

Cayce's clairvoyance, impregnated as it was through and through with religious content and associations, has not a few specific antecedents in the history of Judeo-Christian spirituality. In the Bible itself we have only limited data by which to discern the psychological mechanism by means of which the consequences of historic Hebrew prophecy emerged. The biblical witness identifies perhaps only three modes of altered states of consciousness by which prophets received their communications—as they believed—from the Lord God, or from him but through his angels. These are dreams, visions, and the "still small voice" (I Kings 19:12). But possibly it would be well to expand the range of this terminology by adding what we may call unusual insight or intuition. All the prophets identified in the Bible as authentic seem to have been characterized by this "gift" of paranormal insight. For persons of faith the entire process could be summed up by the term "divine revelation."

The prophets of the Old Testament were perceived as seers, as forthtellers of the word of God for their time and place. They were, however, also foretellers of the future in the context of the needs of that time and place. Indeed we may say that there is no prophet in the Old Testament who was not in some measure a foreteller of the future as well as a forthteller of the word of God. For Deutero-Isaiah a distinguishing mark of an authentic prophet seems to have been this ability to foretell the future; it was the basis of his claim to speak with the authority of Yahweh, who alone knows the future but reveals it to those whom he chooses (compare Isa. 41:21–23; 42:9).

This, of course, is the language of faith, but such language—the classification of clairvoyant perception as revelation—becomes legitimately possible only in the context of religious faith, of religious tradition as the heritage of an ongoing religious community, and of a disciplined lifestyle on the part of the prophet himself that is recognized by the community as authentic. Let us inquire briefly how this process worked.

The daily necessity to make qualitative evaluations of persons and events, as of things, is central to human life. Such evaluation, of course, is all the more necessary in the case of religious teachers or alleged prophets, who purport to communicate truth of cosmic significance. Jesus taught his disciples to evaluate religious teachers by their fruits in conduct. He did not allow social acceptance or professions of faith or sincerity to have primary significance in the process of evaluation (compare Matt. 7:15–23; 12:33–35; 25:31–46; Luke 6:43–45; John 14:11; 1 John 2:29). (As we move from the recorded teaching of Jesus to the apostolic writings of the New Testament, the criteria of religious evaluation come to include theological as well as ethical criteria.)

The Hebrew prophet Jeremiah employed this same criterion as primary in his own need to evaluate the contemporary "false prophets" in Judah. They not only opposed and contradicted him, they outnumbered him, they had superior social acceptance and status, and they were in the formal sense as much "Hebrew of the Hebrews" as he was (compare Jer. 23:14–22).

In Jeremiah's case the process of evaluation was evidently a primary need for the sake first of establishing his authenticity as a prophet in his own eyes. But the same process, with the same set of criteria, functioned in the case of the larger community. That is, the final evaluation of a prophet's authenticity before God and in the light of his tradition was made on the basis of the moral quality of his teaching and of his life, as well as on the basis of whether both teaching and life were in essential conformity to the tradition—even when some modifications or corrections of the tradition were made, an aspect of the prophetic ministry of both Jeremiah and Jesus (compare Jer. 31:26–34; Matt. 5:21–48).

This process seems to have functioned as the primary means by which all the Hebrew prophets included in the biblical records came to be recognized as authentic by the collective judgment of their community of faith. The same process is also at work in the New Testament in the frequent apostolic injunctions to discern the spirits, a phrase used to indicate discernment of the dominant quality of a person's character, or more specifically, the quality of a supernal force at work in the lives of individuals or of a community of faith (compare 1 Cor. 2:14; 12:10; 1 Thess. 5:19–22; 1 John 4:1, also Matt. 16:3; 1 Cor. 11:29; and the extracanonical *Didache* 11:8–12).

I do not intend to suggest that Edgar Cayce is to be classified as a prophet precisely in the same sense as the prophets of the Hebrew tradition. His own claims were distinctly more modest. In the more than forty years of his clairvoyant activity Cayce never, or almost never, prefaced his statements (whether from his conscious mind or from an altered state of consciousness) with the words, "Thus saith the Lord." The prophets recorded in the Old Testament, on the other hand, often used this or similar phrases to indicate their belief that what they were saying was the veritable word of God. Their acceptance as authentic prophets both by their immediate disciples and ultimately by the larger community of faith was predicated upon acceptance of this kind of prophetic claim. Cayce, however, did not advance the claim to be a spokesman of the word of God in this direct way. To the contrary, a distinct modesty and reserve characterized his self-description at this point.

Yet the readings do claim to speak the truth, even though they frequently ask that hearers, or readers, apply and test this truth in their personal life experience and correlate the content with other appropriate data, supremely with the Judeo-Christian Scriptures. The Cayce *life* readings, especially, are thus properly to be viewed as twentieth-century devotional material that can be used as guides for the daily life of faith in the context of regular reading of the Bible and ongoing participation in the life and service of a worshiping community of faith. Hence the methodology of this book as a comparative study.

Among other examples of communication of specific knowledge from alleged higher sources, we may note the instance in one of the biblical Apocrypha of medical knowledge cited as given by revelation from an angel of the Lord (Tobit 6:1–8). We may also appropriately recall instances in the history of Christian spirituality whereby details of the life of Jesus beyond those recorded in the Bible have been given through various kinds of visionary experience. We may cite as examples St. Catherine of Siena (1347–1380), Anne Catherine Emmerich (1774–1824), Rudolf Steiner (1861–1925), and Therese Neumann of more recent times (1898–1962). Anne Catherine Emmerich and Therese Neumann were German Roman Catholic nuns whose clairvoyant activity has been carefully studied by numerous specialists and given respectful attention both within and without their church. With reference to responsible—cautious but considerate—ecclesiastical evaluation of data of this kind, and of the persons who are the instruments of their communication, I know of no better treatment than an essay written by the French Roman Catholic Abbé de Cazales in the nineteenth century. This essay appears in English as the preface to the book, *The Dolorous Passion of Our Lord Jesus Christ*, on the life and work of Sr. Emmerich.

We have a specific example similar in methodological procedure to Edgar Cayce's in none other than Thomas Aquinas (1225–1274), who is almost universally regarded as the greatest systematic theologian of the High Middle Ages in Western Europe. Aquinas's early biographers drew also upon the testimony of his personal secretaries. In *Friar Thomas D'Aquino, His Life, Thought and Work*, James A. Weisheipl, O.P., gives the report of one of these—a Breton named Evan Garnit—that ''Thomas after dictating to him and two other secretaries, would sometimes sit down to rest from the work and, falling asleep, would go on dictating in his sleep; Evan meanwhile continuing to write just the same.''

A final word may be given from the work of the Icelandic social scientist Erlendur Haraldsson, who devoted ten years of his life and made ten journeys to India to investigate the contemporary Indian religious teacher and alleged miracle-worker Sathya Sai Baba (b. 1926). Haraldsson has noted in his book *Modern Miracles* that in the larger scientific community—including the social sciences together with natural sciences—there are at least two ways of apprehending truth. One is the way of *experimental* science, the other is the method of *descriptive* science. Haraldsson reminds us that our judicial systems have developed the methodology of interrogation and corroboration of witnesses, along with the investigation of pertinent documentation and the like, as proper and reliable modes of gaining and establishing evidence. This methodology belongs of course to the category of descriptive science, as do all the procedures of research in the social sciences, including history—and theology.

Our own investigation of the Edgar Cayce readings belongs, I believe, in the same category of descriptive science. All scientific research, furthermore, in the natural sciences as well as in the social, tries to develop its hypotheses on the basis of as large a quantity of data as possible. In the case of our judicial system, given the selective and at times biased—as well as fallible—nature of human memory, the courts normally rely on quantity of testimony and on the consesus of numerous witnesses. We are able to do something akin to this, I believe, in our present study of the life and teachings of Jesus the Christ as given in the Edgar Cayce readings as we use the large number of readings available and correlate them with other related data.

Edgar Cayce gave a total of 14,256 readings, from the earliest dated reading in 1909 until his death on January 3, 1945. A point of primary significance in this large corpus of materials, apart from their great quantity, is their internal consistency. An appreciable number of persons received more than one reading, sometimes with an interval of ten years or more between one discourse and the next. Yet the historical, cosmological, and ethico-religious materials given on these occasions—often in very different personal and historical settings as well as years apart—show such a rigorous consistency as to cause amazement. This astonishing consistency of content is also evident when readings given for particular persons are compared, again often years apart. But even more significant than logical or factual consistency—important as these are—is the internal moral and religious quality of these materials. As you read on in this study you will be able to judge for yourself as to this quality in the case of the materials on Jesus the Christ.

A LIFE OF
JESUS
THE CHRIST

Part I

THE BIRTH AND EARLY YEARS

1

THE COSMIC BACKGROUND

THE PREEXISTENCE OF Jesus the Christ is a faith-theme emphasized by several writers in the New Testament. The term "preexistence" is used to indicate the belief that the man Jesus of Nazareth did not begin his existence as a being in this universe with his birth from the virgin Mary at the start of our present Common Era; rather, Jesus existed from the beginning of the universe in a special relationship with God the Father that is described in several ways in the New Testament.

We find this concept in the prologue of the Gospel of John, where Jesus is proclaimed as the preexistent Logos (Word) who became a true human being (John 1:1–18). The Apostle Paul expresses the concept in classic form in his letter to the Philippians, where he writes of Christ Jesus as having been in the "form" of God but emptied himself to become human and serve the saving purposes of God toward humanity (Phil. 2:1–11). The writer of the letter to the Hebrews sees Jesus as the pioneer of human salvation, the Son through whom God created the world, who yet "for a little while was made lower than the angels . . . so that by the grace of God he might taste death for every one" (Heb. 1:2; 2:9; compare I Pet. 1:20).

It is not so well known that a number of early Jewish Christian groups handled the theme somewhat differently.

According to Epiphanius, in *Adversus Haereses*, the Jewish Christian Ebionites taught that the Spirit, whom they considered superior to the angels and yet able to descend to the earth as he willed, had come as Adam and was later reincarnated as Jesus. The influence of the Ebionites reached beyond the Transjordan area and extended over a large part of south-western Asia well into the fourth century A.D. Hippolytus, an early Christian writer, claims that another Jewish Christian sect, the Elkasaites, taught that when Jesus was born of a virgin he was not making his first appearance on earth. He had been incarnated previously, the same soul being born in different bodies at different times and places. The so-called pseudo-Clementine writings (which are generally classed as later forms of authentic second-century witness to Jewish Christianity) indicate belief in a series of incarnations of Jesus prior to his manifestation as the Christ in Palestine at the beginning of our era.

According to the Clementine *Homilies*, the soul—whom the Apostle Paul calls the firstborn of all creation (Rom. 8: 29; Col. 1:15; compare Heb. 2:11)—was incarnated as Adam, then as Enoch, Noah, Abraham, Isaac, Jacob, Moses, and finally as Jesus. The Edgar Cayce readings, which in a number of ways are theologically akin to early Jewish Christianity as to the great Alexandrian theologians Clement and Origen, give us a list similar in principle, different in details. The Cayce list is Adam, Enoch, Melchizedek, Joseph, Joshua, Jeshua (the scribe responsible, according to Cayce, for the work of collection of sacred writings leading to the later form of the Hebrew Bible) and Jesus (no. 5749–14).*

---

*Each of the Edgar Cayce readings has been assigned a two-part number to provide easy reference. Each person who received a reading was given an anonymous number; this is the first half of the two-part number. Since many individuals obtained more than one reading, the second number designates the number of that reading in the series. Reading no. 5749–14 was given for a person who was assigned case number 5749. This particular reading was the fourteenth one this person obtained from Cayce. Scripture references in the readings are to the King James version of the English Bible.

Thus the Cayce readings espouse the concept of reincarnation, the notion that the same entity or soul may experience repeated lives on earth, and, like many early Jewish Christians, apply the concept as descriptive of the preexistence of Jesus.

This concept of reincarnation was widely believed in the larger Hellenistic society at the time of Jesus, specifically in the line of the Pythagorean and Platonic philosophical tradition. Many Jews also held to some form of this view. The Alexandrian Jewish historian Flavius Josephus, a later contemporary of Jesus, tells us (in his *Jewish War III, Against Apion II*, and *Jewish Antiquities XVIII*) that the Pharisees believed good souls return to earth in bodies. Indeed, if one is willing to accept the literal meaning of the text in Matt. 17:9–13, it appears that Jesus himself believed that John the Baptizer was the reincarnation of the Old Testament prophet Elijah (compare Matt. 11:11–15, John 1:21).

The concept of reincarnation in the Edgar Cayce readings is held to apply to all human beings. It stresses the educative nature and purposes of the human experiences: "Each sojourn or indwelling may be compared to . . . a lesson, as a schooling for the purposes for which each soul-entity enters in earth experience" (no. 1158–5); In *A Search for God II*, a rephrase of a Cayce reading says "Our entrance into the earth plane at any time is for the purpose that another lesson may be gained, another opportunity for soul expression may be had."

This understanding is similar to that of the Alexandrian theologian Origen (ca. 185–253/4), the most learned biblical scholar and probably the single most influential theologian in the first six centuries of the history of the Christian church. Origen believed this material world to be beautiful and good, the creation of a beneficent God. "But it is not comfortable and is not intended to be." Human beings are born here for ultimately spiritual and moral purposes. That is, we are given educational opportunities that we may return to fellowship with our Maker and to working harmony with his plan.

Origen also taught reincarnation as a "very plausible opinion." He felt that the inequalities and apparent injustices of life on earth could be rightly understood only on the assumption that souls preexist and are given bodies and circumstances—which also constitute our appropriate opportunities for personal transformation and growth—in consequence of the actions of our previous lives. According to Henry Chadwick, in *Early Christian Thought and the Classical Tradition,* Origen held this concept to be "absolutely necessary to any persuasive theodicy."

We should also note that according to one of the letters of Jerome (ca. 340–420; the translator of the Hebrew and Greek Bible into the Latin Vulgate), belief in reincarnation was widely held by Christians in his own time, especially in the churches of the Greek-speaking areas bordering on the eastern Mediterranean Sea.

The Edgar Cayce readings, therefore, like the writings of many fathers in the early Christian church, view the Christ event as occurring in the context of a panorama of divine purpose and activity cosmically vast in range but unified in nature. God is described in the Cayce readings with rich profusion of predicates or epithets. Typical examples include the following: "God, the Father, the Universal Influence, the Creative Energy, the I AM THAT I AM" (no. 262–87); "Life is an essence of the Father" (no. 5749–4); "God is love, hence occupies a space, place, condition, and is the Force that permeates all activity" (no. 5749–4).

In the beginning, we are told, God "moved." God from the beginning could be called multiple, as well as unitive; for "in the beginning was the Word, the Word was God, the Word was with God." As God moved, "souls—portions of Himself—came into being" (no. 262–13; compare John 1: 1).

"Ye are part and parcel of a Universal Consciousness or God—and thus [of] all that is within the universal Consciousness, or the Universal Awareness" (no. 2974–3). In the Cayce readings, however, this perception by no means can be classified as constituting pantheism or philosophical monism in the strict sense of the terms. The distinctive relationship of the soul (as a part) to God (as the Whole) is revealed in the following quotation, given in answer to the question of the purpose of an entity's existence:

> That it, the entity, may *know* itself to *be* itself, and part of the Whole; not the Whole but one *with* the Whole; and thus retaining its individuality, knowing itself to be itself yet one with the purposes of the First Cause that willed it, the entity, into *being,* into the awareness, into the consciousness of itself. That is the purpose, that is the cause of *being.* (no. 826–11)

This concept of God creating souls as akin to himself in nature and therefore being a derivative part of himself is given in many readings with somewhat varying expressions but essentially identical meaning (compare Acts 17:28). It constitutes a subtle variation of the usual doctrine of creation. It is not emanation, as if the process were automatic and without divine conscious purpose and act. The readings forthrightly affirm divine creation and use the term. In a sense there was a "point" or "time" when souls, as separate foci of consciousness or awareness, did not exist. But since they participate in consciousness as the primary element of their nature, they are of the same nature as God, although derivatively so. Furthermore all individual souls or entities now in existence, whether living on earth or in other realms, are stated to have been created "in the beginning" (no. 5749–14). We have the further statement that "man was created a little bit higher than all the rest of the whole universe, and is capable of harnessing, directing, enforcing, the laws of the universe" (no. 5–2; compare Heb. 2:6–8; Ps. 8:4–6). This then is the high anthropology of the Edgar Cayce readings, its high view of what it means to be a human being. With this view we must conjoin also their high christology, their view, truly exalted, of the person and work of Jesus the

Christ. This high christology includes a further point of great significance regarding the wider work and influence of Jesus on the historical plane during the purported earlier incarnations. It also includes work and influence from spiritual realms between incarnations, activity that works with heightened effectiveness after the Christ event, by which the entity who was born as Jesus in Bethlehem became one with the Christ and potentially accessible to every human being in every time and place. We learn that earlier "the entity—as an entity—influenced either directly or indirectly all those forms of philosophy or religious thought that taught God was One" (no. 364–9); "In all those periods that the basic principle was the Oneness of the Father, He has walked with men" (no. 364–8).

We should note that this twofold mode of influence—working on the plane of history and from higher dimensions—has not, according to the Cayce readings, been confined to the people of Israel and the Christian church. We read that the entity who became Jesus "associated with—in the meditation or spirit of"—Gautama the Buddha (no. 364–9). These words should be interpreted, I believe, in the context of understanding that the Buddha's perception of the Dharma—as the central element of his faith-object and worldview—was such that we may properly include him in the category of those who taught that God is One. In the same way that many things have been added to the original expressions of Judaism, much has been added to Confucianism, Buddhism, Platonism, and Islam "from that as was given by Jesus in His walk in Galilee and Judea. In all of these, then, there is that same impelling spirit" (no. 364–9). Another expression of this theme is found in the 262 series of readings given for the group that produced the two volumes of *A Search for God,* which have served long and well as the working basis for study groups across this country and the world. This is that Jesus "has led in all of the experiences of thought in *any* of the presented forms of truth in the earth, and comes at last to the cross" (no. 262–34).

This theme is further explained in a later reading in the same series, which states that the soul of Jesus also

> through the varying activities overcame the world through the *experiences*, bearing the cross in each and every experience, reaching the *final* cross with *all* power, *all* knowledge in having overcome the world—and of Himself *accepted* the cross. Hence doing away with that often termed Karma, that must be met by all. (no. 262–36; compare Matt. 11:27; 28:18; Gal. 6:7)

It is important for us to realize that the Cayce readings in this way are attempting to give some specific content to the ancient Christian belief in the preexistence of Jesus. The contention is that the great being who as Jesus of Nazareth became the Christ was active in revealing, in teaching the truth of God from higher realms to the hearts and minds of human beings throughout human history. The affirmation is further made that in previous incarnations upon the earth Jesus, in ever higher progression of his own spiritual development and of service to others, bore the cross of suffering and thus overcame the negative effects of the past of himself and of others (compare no. 262–82). This was all to the end of coming to "the final cross," whereby Jesus fully overcame the world and completed the process that provides redemption, liberation, reconciliation to all.

2

THE HISTORICAL PREPARATIONS FOR THE BIRTH OF JESUS

THE EDGAR CAYCE readings affirm in the clearest terms and with strong emphasis that the "man called Jesus" lived a real human life. We read that "this man, as man, makes the will the will of the Father, then becoming one with the Father and the model for man" (no. 900–10). Furthermore the strongest language is used to assert Jesus' manifestation in flesh and blood and the reality of his physical as well as mental suffering on the cross as also before (notably in the Garden of Gethsemane).

The birth of the man Jesus is seen in the Cayce readings as the final state of the earthly development of the one who became the supreme instrument of the Father's work for the salvation (reconciliation-restoration of personal relationships and transformation-development of character) of all humankind. This process of personal growth-development, however, is seen as one in which all human beings must also participate—through realms both earthly and transearthly, with an earthly incarnation required as a part of each particular stage of development (no. 900–16). Jesus is described in the Cayce readings as "the soul who first went through the cycle of earthly lives to attain perfection, including perfection in the planetary lives also" (no. 5749–14). And his work as Jesus the Christ is said to be "a voluntary mission [on the part of] One who was already perfected and returned to God, having accomplished His Oneness in other planes and systems'' (no. 5749–14). (In this context we may properly recall the words of the letter to the Hebrews [5:8–9]: ''Although he was a Son, he learned obedience through what he suffered; and being made perfect he became the source of eternal salvation to all who obey him, being designated by God a high priest after the order of Melchizedek.'') This background was essential for the ''manifestation in the earth of the holy influence for the sustaining of a backsliding world'' (no. 5749–3). He came through his own choice—as well as being sent (no. 5749–7).

The Cayce readings affirm that preparations were also being made on the historical plane within the history of Israel. The primary focus of these preparations properly to prepare the way and receive the Holy One was seen by Cayce to lie within the religious sect or school of the Jews called the Essenes, which like other contemporary sects in Israel had its ''adherents and near adherents'' (no. 1602–4).

Something of the nature of this religious community has long been known through the writings of Josephus, who in fact seems to have considered them a nobler lot than either the Pharisees or Sadducees. This sect has become the object of considerable public as well as academic interest and study since the discovery of the first Qumran (also called Dead Sea) Scrolls in 1947, for the scrolls are generally held to be the product of the Essene community. It is significant that the Cayce readings indicated as early as June 22, 1937, the existence as well as the location of the Qumran community and specifically identified them as Essenes.

According to the Edgar Cayce readings the primary purpose of the spiritual activity of the Essenes was to raise up persons who would be fit channels for the birth of the Messiah (no. 262–61). Their tradition was said to be in the direct line of spiritual descent from the school of prophets established by Elijah, although in a sense this activity stems back to the earlier charismatic prophet Samuel, who in turn allegedly drew upon the teachings of Melchizedek. Surprisingly the readings contend that the Essenes, at least in the period just prior to the birth of Jesus, "took Jews and Gentiles alike as members" (no. 254–109). The Essenes are also said to have had notable international associations, and for this as for other reasons were regarded as unorthodox by the rabbis of this period (no. 2067–11).

The Essenes are also said in the Cayce readings to have had a special connection with Mount Carmel from the time of Elijah. It is significant that the present Carmelite Order of the Roman Catholic church has preserved a tradition of the Eastern Orthodox monastics who had long lived on Mount Carmel and who welcomed as brothers in faith and practice the monks who came from western Europe with the Crusaders. According to an essay by Robert F. Adriance in Violet M. Shelley's *Journey to Mount Carmel,* the tradition asserts that their order had in fact been founded by Elijah, and that with the name of the Sons of the prophets they had made their preparations for the birth of the Messiah. When the Messiah came, in the person of Jesus, they accepted him as such and continued to live on Mount Carmel, becoming in time a recognized monastic order in the Eastern Orthodox church. From the union of this ancient lineage with the monks from the West there developed, the tradition claims, the present Carmelite Order.

The Cayce readings state that Mary and Joseph and Mary's cousin Elizabeth were all members of the Essene community of faith and raised their children in that context and mode. We are told that Zechariah, the husband of Elizabeth, as a member of the orthodox priesthood—that is, a priest according to the Aaronic line—was not at first an Essene but became at least a sympathizer toward the end of his life, as the result of his visions in the temple (compare Luke 1:5–23). The readings also identify this same Zechariah, the father of John the Baptizer, with the Zechariah who is said in the biblical accounts to have been murdered "between the sanctuary and the altar" (Matt. 23:35; Luke, 11:51). They state that the murder occurred precisely because of Zechariah's open proclamation of the content of his visions and, presumably, because such proclamation signified a commitment to the Essene position (no. 5749–8). The content was evidently a prophecy of the coming Messianic events largely according to the expectations of the Essenes (no. 2167–1).

The readings, particularly the 5749 series requested by Thomas Sugrue, are richly detailed in their description of the process of preparation for the birth of the Christ Child. They culminate in a description of the selection and training of Mary and, of course, in accounts of the birth itself. The Cayce readings not only affirm the virgin birth of Jesus, but also state—going even beyond ancient Eastern tradition—that Mary herself was born of a virgin, that her mother Anne bore her without a human father (no. 5749–7,8). The Cayce readings also affirm that Mary, like Jesus, was "without original sin from the moment of her conception in the womb" (no. 5749–8). This is in effect to confirm the correctness of the Roman Catholic dogma of the Immaculate Conception of Mary. This dogma, as defined by Pope Pius IX on December 8, 1854, refers not to birth from a virgin but to freedom from original sin from the moment of conception.

The readings state that as part of the preparation for the coming of the Messiah into materiality the Essene leaders determined to select and train twelve young girls as potential channels. "In Carmel—where there were the priests of this faith [Essene]—there were the maidens chosen that were dedicated to this purpose, this office" (no. 5749–7). At this time Mary was only four years old. She was, however, "between twelve and thirteen" (5749–8) when she was designated as the one who was to be the specific physical channel for the coming of the Master. The training of the twelve maidens comprised physical, mental, and spiritual dimensions, including "chastity, purity, love, patience, endurance" (no. 5749–8), as well as proper diet.

It was a discipline that could be called severe for the sake of physical and mental strength. The focus of this training was the temple of the Essenes on Mount Carmel.

According to Cayce the Essene decision to choose Mary
was made primarily on the basis of a singularly beautiful
angelic visitation one morning as the maidens were proceed-
ing to the altar for prayer and the burning of incense (no.
5749–8). From this time onward Mary was "separated and
kept in closer associations . . ." (no. 5749–7) with the teachers and mentors responsible for her training. The Cayce readings assert that in this event or series of events may be
discerned the beginning of the Christian church (no. 4749–
7).

Mary is said to have been "between sixteen and seventeen
[when] she was found with child" (no. 5749–8), and thus
there was a further period of training "of some three to four
years" from the time of her final designation until the conception (no. 5749–8). Joseph's age is given as thirty-six at
the time of their marriage, with the rite being performed in
the Essene temple on Mount Carmel. Joseph was selected
from the priests of the Essenes as a "chosen vessel" for this
role (no. 5749–7).

Mary and Joseph had previously known each other to the
extent normal for fellow members of disparate ages belonging to the same religious community (no. 5749–9). The marriage was in a sense "arranged"; but, according to the Cayce
readings, the leaders of the Essene community played a role
in this arrangement beyond what was usual (the parents of
the contracting parties were commonly the dominant factors
in the decision process [no. 5749–8]).

Both Mary and Joseph consented to the arrangement, but
the readings state that Joseph at first demurred at the suggestion of the Essene leaders that he become the husband of
Mary. This hesitancy was in part because of Joseph's awe
as one well aware of Essene expectations that Mary would
become the mother of the Messiah. To my knowledge the
Cayce readings nowhere state that the Essenes expected the
birth of the Messiah to be virginal. In fact they state that it
was not generally believed in the Essene community that
Mary's birth from Anne had been virginal (no. 5749–8, A-

2). Therefore it came as a surprise to Joseph, as well as to the others, that Mary became pregnant before the marriage had been been consummated (5749–8, A-9). This was indeed a "conception through the Holy Spirit" (no. 1158–5).

An additional part of Joseph's concern lay in what public opinion would say about the disparity in their ages. He agreed to the Essene request, the readings say, only after he had confirmation through his own personal religious experience—first in a dream and then by a "direct voice" experience—that the marriage was indeed according to the will of God (no. 5749–8). The readings also indicate that Joseph not only had initial hesitancy about the proposed plan but, as in the biblical account, felt consternation when Mary was found to be with child while yet a virgin. He cooperated with the Essene program here, too, only after his own religious experience gave him confirmation (compare Matt. 1:18–25).

The Cayce readings, while they unequivocally affirm the virgin birth of both Jesus and Mary, do not support the doctrine of the "perpetual virginity" of Mary, which even Martin Luther favored. The readings assert that for about ten years after the birth of Jesus—while he was still under their roof and in their care—Mary and Joseph did not have conjugal relations. But after Jesus' departure for further training by the Essenes and later, as we shall see, in other lands, they took up the normal sexual life of a married couple (no. 5749–8, A-12, 15).

The Essenes, according to the Cayce readings, had a higher conception of the position and role of women in human life than was common among the Jews of the time (no. 254–104). They clearly had prophetesses as well as prophets among their leaders. This Essene outlook thus constitutes a specific background for the fuller development seen in "the teaching of Jesus, that released woman from that bondage to which she had been held since the ideas of man conceived from the fall of Eve or of her first acceptance of the opinions" (no. 2067–11). In this connection Jesus the Christ is not to be seen as merely a projection of his Essene background. A comparison with his cousin, John the Baptizer, specifically stated that "John was more the Essene than Jesus. For Jesus held rather to the spirit of the law, and John to the letter of same" (no. 2067–1).

This then was the background of the birth of "the Savior, the Messiah, the Prince of Peace, the Way, the Truth, the Light" (no. 1010–17); "that beloved Son, who would make the paths straight, who would bring *man out* of darkness into light . . . that Shepherd [who] must lead forth His flock, His brethren again into the light of the countenance of an all-merciful Father" (no. 587–6). The purpose of the birth of Jesus was clearly divine. "The purpose of the entrance of the Son *into* the earth [was] that man might have the closer walk with, yea the open door to, the very heart of the living God!" (no. 587–6; compare Mark 12:29; Deut. 6:4).

3
THE BIRTH

THE EDGAR CAYCE readings give two main dates for the birth of the Christ Child: the twenty-fourth/twenty-fifth of December (no. 5749-8)—the birth occurred "just as the midnight hour came" (no. 5949-15); and the sixth of January. These two dates have historically been celebrated by the two major branches of the Christian church, the Western (including the Roman Catholic and Protestant churches) and the Eastern Orthodox churches. The readings state that each date has a legitimate basis, depending on the calendar used or the period in which calculation is made. (Another reading affirms that the date of Jesus' birth was March 19 in the year A.D. 4, a calculation based on the use of the Julian calendar, or the year 1899, based on the Mosaic calendar (no. 587-6). Whether these differences can be reconciled, I am unable to say.)

Mary and Joseph arrived in Bethlehem in the evening, the readings state, and the weather was cool. There were crowds of people on the way, many from the surrounding hills of Judea, others from the north. Their occupations were varied: shepherds, husbandmen of other kinds of flocks, farmers, and different kinds of craftsmen. Some in the group from Nazareth are said to be "helpers to Joseph—carpenters' helpers" (no. 5749-15). A number of the readings affirm that Joseph was a carpenter-builder of some means and standing in the community.

The Cayce readings suggest that on their journey to Bethlehem—a trip necessitated by the Roman requirement for each Jew to return to his ancestral place of origin to be registered for tax purposes (compare Luke 2:1–5)—Mary and Joseph may have been accompanied by some of their fellow Essenes. At least they found a number of concerned friends already there when they arrived at the inn, and all shared in the consternation when it was heard that there was no room for the couple. Reading no. 5749–15 gives this account:

> [They had been told] no room in the inn . . . They began to seek some place, some shelter . . .
>
> Thus many joined in the search for some place. Necessity demanded that some place be sought quickly. Then it was found, under the hill, in the stable—above which the shepherds were gathering their flocks into the fold.
>
> There the Savior, the Child was born, who, through the will and the life manifested, became the Savior of the world—that channel through which those of old had been told that the promise would be fulfilled that was made to *Eve* [compare Gen. 3:15], the arising again of another like unto Moses, and as given to David, the promise was not to depart from that channel. But lower and lower man's concept of needs had fallen.
>
> Then—when hope seemed gone—the herald angels sang. The star appeared that made the wonderment to the shepherds, that caused the awe and consternation to all of those about the inn . . .

Like the account in the Gospel of Luke (2:8–20), the Cayce readings affirm the historical reality of the story of the shepherds in the fields at the time of the birth of the Christ Child. Reading no. 587–6 states that the experience of the shepherds in hearing "that cry of the heavenly hosts" was a reflection of the fact that not only all the heavenly hosts but also "all nature . . . proclaimed that glorious period for man" (compare Isa. 9:6). This reading rather poetically states that "all nature—the face in the water, the dew upon tint and the beauty of the rose, the song of the stars, the mourn of the wind, all proclaim—*now*—the mighty words of a merciful, a loving God."

The shepherds are now described as those "who heard the cry of 'Glory to God in the Highest—Peace on earth and good will to men' " (no. 1815–1; compare Luke 2:14); now as those "who heard the voice, who saw the light and who experienced the choir of the angelic hosts that pronounced His advent" (no. 2562–1).

The Cayce readings give relatively detailed accounts of the Wise Men (Magi) who appear briefly but significantly in the Gospel according to Matthew (no. 2:1–23). The fullness of these accounts is due to several reasons. One is that, according to the readings, the Wise Men were concrete representatives of the international contacts of the Essenes and symbols of the wider meaning of the birth of the Christ Child. This was not a geographically local or ethnically restricted occurrence; it was an event of international, historical, and indeed cosmic significance.

The three Wise Men came "with their ladened beasts or camels" (no. 1152–3) from Persia, India, and Egypt. The readings insist, however, that they were later joined by a fourth and a fifth Wise Man, followed by a second group. These men were among the sages, or wise and holy persons, who came from Chaldea, the Gobi Desert area, and what is now Southeast Asia (no. 2067–7; no. 587–6). They were seekers after truth. In particular they were looking for "this happening" (no. 5749–7), for "the day, the hour when that *great purpose*, that event, was to be in the earth a literal experience" (no. 1908–1). They came "to do honor, to give of their substance . . ." (no. 587–6) and to pray "blessings . . . upon the Infant in the manger" (no. 5749–2). They found "the place 'where the child was' " (no. 5749–7) by applying those forces that today would be termed psychic.

The Cayce readings specify also that the tradition of the Persian sages included the study of mathematics, of astronomy and astrology and the other laws of nature (no. 5749–7; no. 1908–1). In Persia "the studies were of the influence of stellar space or the sojourn of souls in the environs about the earth that made—and make—for the mental urges in the souls of men" (no. 256–5). This sentence gives expression to an understanding of the nature of human beings frequently affirmed in the Cayce readings. The "mental urges" that seem to be a part of the experience of every human being are not the results of heredity and environment alone, nor of arbitrary divine creation, nor mere on-the-spot upsurges of feeling with no real cause. They are to a substantial extent the result of each entity's past choices and activities in both earthly and other realms. We may note that in the early Buddhist community the term *Samskara* was used to denote predispositions or habitual tendencies of character that inhere and condition (but not absolutely or irretrievably) a given state of sentient beings as the result of past deeds and experiences.

The Cayce readings are clear in their insistence that the Wise Men had previous contacts with the Jews, in particular with the Essenes. And the Essenes had on their side been drawing upon the spiritual traditions of Persia "as handed down by the old Persian teacher Zoroaster" (no. 1297–1). (There is an almost universal consensus among biblical scholars of the present generation that Persian (Iranian) influence upon the development of Judaism, from the fifth century B.C. and perhaps earlier, is undeniable. One Cayce reading states that the Wise Men came not only with material gifts but also with spiritual teachings [no. 1581–1].) Also of significance is the Cayce assertion that it was the Romans who gave the order for the Wise Men to be conducted to the place that they sought (1220–1).

The Cayce readings agree with the account in the Gospel

of Matthew that King Herod was deeply concerned about what the birth of the child the Wise Men were seeking might portend for the security of his own royal position. The Matthew story is graphic in its depiction of Herod's rage and ferocity, culminating in an order to kill all the male children in the area of Bethlehem who were two years old or under (Mt. 2:1–23). The readings state that the Romans attempted, apparently without success, to halt this killing of babes (no. 1220–1). This, then, is the frightful situation that led Joseph and Mary to take their newborn child and flee to Egypt, a flight specifically dictated, according to the biblical account, by the appearance of an angel to Joseph in a dream (Matt. 2:13).

4

THE FLIGHT TO EGYPT

THE CAYCE READINGS state that the flight of the Holy Family to Egypt was indeed in fulfillment of Old Testament prophecy (no. 5749–16; no. 1010–23; compare Matt. 2:13–33; Hos. 11:1). Only male children of the lineage of David in the territory of Judah were killed (775–1), and the search of Herod's soldiers was for children of the "age from six months to two years" (no. 1010–1).

The readings also say that the decision to flee to Egypt was made in consultation with leaders of the Essene community. In consequence specific plans and preparations were made for the physical protection and care of the family. Both Mary and the infant Jesus were assigned, according to Cayce, to the care of an Essene woman named Josie. For the larger physical protection required "there were other groups [of Essenes] that preceded and followed" the movement of the Holy Family itself.

The flight "began on an evening, and the journey— through portions of Palestine, from Nazareth to the borders of Egypt—was made only during the night ... the period of sojourn in Egypt was in and about, or close to, what was then Alexandria," the duration "a period of some four years—four years, six months, three days. . . . Josie and Mary were not idle during that period of sojourn" in Egypt. In addition to care of the child Jesus, Josie and the parents gave some time to study of records "preserved in portions of the libraries" in Alexandria (no. 1010–17).

The libraries of Alexandria were the result of a program and process initiated in the beginning of the third century B.C. by Ptolemy I, one of the generals of Alexander the Great. They were largely destroyed in the third and fourth centuries A.D. by both accident and anti-intellectual design. Perhaps a half million or more volumes were included in the libraries, mostly in Greek but probably including books (parchments and papyrus scrolls) in other languages. The original ideal was to create an international library that included translations into Greek from the other languages of the Mediterranean coastlands, the Middle East, and even India.

The records that Joseph and Mary studied included what we would today call astrological forecasts. They gave significant details regarding the expected Messiah, even about "the nature of work of the parents . . . their places of sojourn, and the very characteristics that would indicate these individuals." The same reading affirms that the child Jesus "was in every manner a normal, developed body, ready for those activities of children of that particular period," although "the garments worn by the Child would heal children." This statement reminds us of accounts given of miracles wrought by Jesus as a child recorded in the so-called apocryphal gospels (the Cayce readings contain none of the more bizarre stories that are found in some of these gospels). The readings explain the healing power in this phenomenon by stating simply that "the body being perfect radiated that which was health, life itself" and go on to say that even today "individuals may radiate, by their spiritual selves, health, life, that vibration which is destructive to dis-ease in any form in bodies" (no. 1010–17; see also no. 2067–7).

Upon their return to Palestine from Egypt, made relatively safe by the death of King Herod (compare Matt. 2:19–23), the Holy Family went to Capernaum, not to Nazareth, the previous residence of Joseph and Mary. (A brief reference in reading no. 5749–15 suggests that a multiplication of food occurred when an unexpected delay developed en route as the Holy Family was returning to Palestine from Egypt). This is one of the very few instances in which the Cayce readings venture to correct statements of fact given in the Bible (compare Matt. 2:23; Mark 1:9; Luke 2:51). There is reason to believe, however, from the biblical reference in Mark 2:1, that Capernaum was also home to Jesus; it is thus possible that both Nazareth and Capernaum could be called Jesus' home. The Cayce readings do not deny a close relationship between the Holy Family and Nazareth; indeed they frequently refer to Jesus as the Nazarene. After his birth in Bethlehem and the purification of the Mother and the dedication of the Child in the temple in Jerusalem—where the Wise Men were presented to the Mother and allowed to see the Child—the Holy Family is said to have returned to Nazareth. From there they fled to Egypt as a result of Herod's edict (no. 5749–7).

The reasons given by Cayce for the Holy Family's journey to Capernaum were partly political, a result of the Roman division of the administrative area after the death of Herod the Great. But perhaps more important, Capernaum was evidently the proper place for the early instruction of Jesus under the auspices of the Essene community. His instruction there is said to have been supervised by a woman named Judy. Judy appears with considerable prominence in the Cayce readings as the highly respected leader of one group of the Essenes, whose activities are said to have been focused on Mount Carmel and the Essene temple there. It is also stated that Capernaum was the place "where dwelt many of those who were later the closer companions of the Master" (no. 5749–7; compare Mark 1:29). This city was the home of Peter and Andrew, as of other of the disciples of Jesus.

The readings indicate that there were differences or divisions of thought among the Essenes as to whether God's providence allows human freedom within divine order or precludes it. "One held to—that it can happen—the other that God makes it happen'' (no. 2072–15; compare no. 1472–3; no. 2072–15). The worldview of the Cayce readings, however, is consistently that of seeing human beings as possessing freedom of the will to make real choices, a certain leeway within a divinely structured order (no. 3976–29; no. 262–86, A-1; no. 5749–14, A-10). The divine intent or hope, however, with regard to human freedom is ''that each man will live for his fellow man!'' (no. 3976–29). The other aspect of this divine purpose and plan is that each person will be ''one who uses that [his or her own] living soul as a companion with God. That's God's purpose. That should be man's purpose'' (no. 3976–29; compare Mark 23:29–31).

5

THE YEARS OF FURTHER EDUCATION AND PREPARATION

THE CAYCE READINGS state that Jesus lived with his parents until he was twelve and also for certain periods thereafter. For most (perhaps all) of the years after the return from Egypt the family's primary place of residence was Capernaum. From the age of twelve, however (evidently after the experience of "disputing or conversing" with rabbis or teachers in the Temple in Jerusalem [no. 2067–7; compare Luke 2:41–52]), Jesus is said to have begun studies at the home of Judy, who normally lived with her husband and mother in the Mount Carmel area (no. 2067–11). These studies were evidently pursued first at Judy's home and then, at her urging, in other lands from "His twelfth to His fifteenth-sixteenth year" (no. 2067–11).

The readings give us a considerable amount of information about Judy, who was clearly a remarkable person—teacher, healer, prophetess. She is said to have been "the first of women appointed as head of the Essene group" (no. 3175–3). "This was the beginning of the period where women were considered as equals with the men in their activities, in their abilities to formulate, to live, to be channels" (no. 254–109). "In those periods soon after the crucifixion [Judy] not only [gave] comfort to the twelve, to the holy women—and understanding as to how woman was redeemed from a place of obscurity to her place in the activities of the affairs of the

race, of the world, of the empire—yea, of the home itself"
(no. 1472–3).

This is a most significant passage. It affirms that Judy, as
a woman, not only instructed the twelve apostles—who, the
language suggests, perhaps with reference to the role of
women in the new Christian movement, needed such instruction—but was the person who took the already relatively
high position of women in the Essene tradition and gave it
a new theological undergirding and extension as a result of
the cosmically significant events of the crucifixion, resurrection, and ascension of Jesus the Christ. This development
was, of course, in keeping with the teaching and practice of
Jesus himself as recorded in the gospels of the New Testament.

Judy's own education was according to Essene practice
and included studies of "the traditions from many of the
Persian lands and from many of the borders about same"
(no. 1472–3). She continued these studies as an adult, since
an important part of her service to the Essene community
lay in the making and keeping of records. In the course of
this work she "came in contact with the Medes, the Persians,
the Indian influence of authority," and it was in consequence
of the weighing of the traditions of these lands with her own
that she came to "that new understanding" (no. 1472–3).

The long tradition of Greek travelers abroad—from Pythagoras and Solon to Herodotus and Strabo—as well as recent archaeological finds in South India of large quantities
of Roman coins of the period of the early empire, make it
clear that crosscultural communications of this kind were
quite possible. According to J. Edgar Bruns's *The Christian
Buddhism of St. John* there were Buddhist emissaries (mis-
sionaries?) in the eastern Mediterranean in the late Hellenistic period.

The primary content of Judy's teaching of Jesus, according
to the Cayce readings, was the whole range of prophetic literature contained both in the standard Hebrew Scriptures and
in the Essene tradition, with special focus on the prophecies

of the life and work of the Messiah (no. 2067–11). And it was Judy who was primarily responsible in sending Jesus abroad for the completion of his studies and training.

These studies were not merely academic in the modern sense of the word—although this dimension was not lacking—but included spiritual training of the most direct and personal kind. Judy was evidently a spiritual director somewhat akin to those in the later Roman Catholic and Eastern Orthodox churches. She herself is stated to have had a variety of religious experiences, including visitations of angels. Yet the readings affirm with equal emphasis that in her daily life she concerned herself in entirely normal fashion with material-physical needs and realities, including "the faculties and desires for material associations—as indicated in the lack of celibacy" (no. 2067–11).

Contrary to the long-held notion, sometimes verging on the romantic, that Jesus, as the legal son of a poor and presumably not well-educated carpenter, had few opportunities for formal education—we are told Jesus studied abroad "in first India, then Persia, then Egypt" from his thirteenth to his sixteenth year (no. 5749–2). (There is an apparent discrepancy in the different Cayce accounts of the order in which Jesus visited these countries. In one case it is said, as in our text, that he studied "in first India" (no. 5749–2), and in another that, "He went to Persia and then to India" (no. 2067–11). Perhaps the latter statement is merely descriptive of the route, but all accounts agree that Jesus returned to his parents from the East and then went on to Egypt.) One reading states specifically that "it is not, as so oft considered, that the family of the Master lacked material opportunities. For from many sources there had come the opportunities for those in the household of the Master to have the greater training" (no. 1179–7). No doubt the wider resources of the Essene community were made available for this purpose. It is said of Jesus' sister Ruth—so named in the Cayce readings—that she "was educated not only in the best of the land [of Israel] but in other lands" (no. 1179–7). Jesus' own education in Palestinian context, however, like Ruth's later, was clearly according to Essene style, not that of the Pharisees or Sadducees.

The duration of Jesus' schooling in India is given as three years; the period in Persia, including travel, one year. The content of the teachings that he received in India was evidently in keeping with the religious teachings of non-Hebrew peoples as these had been collected and integrated by the Essene schools, a process in which Judy herself had participated; but the teachings were not "the true Essene doctrine as practiced by the Jewish and semi-Jewish associations in Carmel" (no. 2067–7).

The Indian content more particularly had to do with "those cleansings of the body as related to the preparation for strength in the physical as well as in the mental man" (no. 5749–2), a regimen evidently more disciplinary than primarily religious in content. The intent, we learn, was "that there might be completed the more perfect knowledge of the material ways in the activities of Him that became the Way, the Truth" (no. 1472–3). One of Judy's major concerns, however, was that Jesus in his studies abroad should also study "what you would today call astrology" (no. 2067–11). Jesus is said always to have registered under the name Jesua [Yeshua?] in his educational travels (no. 2067–7).

THE NATURE OF JESUS' EDUCATION OUTSIDE PALESTINE

In Persia Jesus' studies and practice are said to have focused on the "unison of forces," physical, mental, and spiritual, according to the traditional teachings in that land. Hence the concern for astrological dimensions of learning, not in its superstitious or fateful sense, but in its primary principle of the interrelatedness of all phenomena. The various Cayce readings that refer to Jesus' educational experiences, "the travels of the Master during the periods of preparation" (no.

5749–7), all seem to suggest a surprisingly broad and inclusive rather than a narrow or sectarian kind of education. Yet they were aimed at culminating in a profound experience that the Cayce readings denote as initiation, an event to be experienced in Egypt.

Jesus' instruction abroad was interrupted, we learn, by the death of Joseph, and he returned to Palestine before going on to Egypt. The Essene nurse Josie's closeness to the family is revealed by the indication that she was present at the death bed and "closed the eyes and laid him to rest" (no. 1010–12). It was from Persia that Jesus was called back home upon the death of Joseph "and then [he went on] into Egypt for the completion of the preparation as a teacher" (no. 5749–7). It was at this point that Jesus' educational experiences converged in a special way with those of his cousin John, who became the Baptizer. "He was with John, the messenger, during the portion of the training there in Egypt" (no. 5749–7). We read that "John first went to Egypt—where Jesus joined him and both became the initiates in the pyramid or temple there" (no. 2067–11).

The Cayce readings state that "as indicated oft through this channel, the unifying of the teachings of many lands was brought together in Egypt, for that was the center from which there was to be the radial activity of influence in the earth" (no. 2067–7). We have already taken note of Greek travelers abroad from an early period. Many of these went to Egypt, as did the Greek statesman and lawgiver Solon in the early sixth century B.C., the philosopher Pythagoras in the late sixth century, and Plato at the beginning of the fourth. The influence of Egyptian civilization as a significant factor in the formation of classical Greece, as in the history of the Hebrews, has generally not been sufficiently recognized. We may profitably recall the words of the first Christian martyr, Stephen, that "Moses was instructed in all the wisdom of the Egyptians" (Acts 7:22).

The initiation of Jesus in Egypt is said to have involved a literal passage through the chamber in the pyramid—evidently the Great Pyramid on the Giza plateau (no. 5748–5; no. 5749–2)—symbolic of the tomb of the soul. This initiation was an external manifestation of what was internally "the crucifying of self in relationships to ideals that make for the abilities of carrying on that called to be done" (no. 5749–2; compare Matt. 4:1–11, 10:38–39, 16:25–26). This emptying of self (compare Phil. 2:1–11) represented the complete and utter dedication of self to the Father and his will (compare Matt. 26:39–44). It was a commitment that according to the Cayce readings was of the essence of Jesus' relationship to the Father and formed the basis of his entire life as of his public ministry. The commitment was in a deep sense both formalized and realized in this initiation experience. The event, therefore, was not an isolated one, divorced either from Jesus' previous training, of which it was in fact the culmination, nor from his subsequent life of obedient service, of which it was the "initiation."

The readings indicate also that Jesus' baptism in the Jordan River by John was a kind of fulfillment in ritual form of his "passing through the initiation" (no. 2067–7; compare Mark 1:1–11). According to the Cayce readings the whole process of Jesus' educational training and spiritual discipline was necessary not only for the perfecting of himself to serve the Father's purposes in behalf of others (compare Mark 10: 45), but also for the fulfillment of his own personal needs. It was, in a word, the recapitulation in reverse (upward rather than downward) of his experience as Adam (no. 2067–7; compare 1 Cor. 15:21–22). Jesus' age at the time was evidently sixteen.

The Cayce reading goes on to say that this kind of initiation, similar in kind if not in form, is "a part of the passage through that to which each soul is to attain in its development. . . . Each entity, each soul, as an initiate" (no. 2067–7) must pass through the same kind of tomb experience in order to obtain its own liberation and final attainment of its goal of being a companion and cocreator with its Maker. The readings emphasize, however, that there was a unique redemptive aspect to Jesus' initiation experience. That is, his initiation constituted also a prefiguration of his later three days and three nights in the tomb (compare Mark 15:46). It is further stated that only Jesus was able to break the power of the tomb, or death. The empty tomb "has *never* been filled" since then (no. 2067–7).

A number of the Cayce readings refer to Jesus as the Great Initiate, who took "those last of the Brotherhood degrees with John, the forerunner of Him, at that place" (no. 5748–5), that is, in the Great Pyramid of Giza. He was "the Great Initiate, the Holy One, the Son of man, the Accepted One of the Father" (no. 5749–2). The readings in effect acknowledge a certain continuity between the so-called Mystery Religions of pre-Christian antiquity at their best and the life experience of Jesus the Christ, in that he participated personally in the traditional rites and at the same time fulfilled them to the end that henceforth in transformed guise they could bear a deeper significance and have greater effects— and that not just for the few, but for all humankind.

These references to initiation and brotherhood degrees may be distasteful to some readers, given the centuries-long tensions between some of the Christian churches and various nonecclesiastical religious orders, such as the Masonic and the Rosicrucian. I would not presume to defend one or the other but simply note that Cayce's statements give us an understanding similar to that of the well-known Austrian philosopher, educator, and clairvoyant mystic Rudolf Steiner (1861–1925). In his *Background to the Gospel of St. Mark* Steiner writes that there was:

> In Jesus of Nazareth, in whom the Christ was present, something which had been witnessed again and again in the Mysteries, but never as an historic reality, yet it was a repetition of the temple rituals. The life of Jesus could therefore have been described by specifying the states passed through in other circumstances during the process of initiation.

Mary and Joseph entered into normal conjugal relations only after Jesus left their household to begin his educational experiences under the guidance and protection of others. According to the readings their ten-year long self-restraint was not from any external requirement; "it was a choice of them both because of their *own* feelings" (no. 5749–8).

But when they began normal associations the children "came in succession: James, the daughter [Ruth], Jude" (no. 5749–8).

The Cayce readings go on to describe some of the feelings of the children, especially of the daughter Ruth, who was born in Capernaum (and evidently raised there; see no. 1179–7), as to what it was like to be born and raised in such a family. The unusual circumstances as well as nature of Jesus' birth were evidently fairly well known, at least among those of Essene affiliation, as indicated in this excerpt:

> There was awe in the minds of the peoples as to what had taken place at the birth of the mother's, or Mary's, first son.
>
> Hence the entity, Ruth, was rather in awe of the suggestions, the intimations that surrounded that experience, and questioned the mother concerning same.
>
> As the entity grew into maidenhood, and after the birth of Jude, then the death of Joseph brought that brother—Jesus—home! And there were those activities that surrounded the entity concerning that unknown, that strange kinsman, that kinsman whom the peoples held in awe, yet said many unkind things about. (no. 1158–4)

The Cayce readings also record some of the doubt and questionings of Ruth concerning her brother Jesus. We are told that she often asked Mary, "How *can* such things be? How *can* He without father come into the world" (no. 1158–9)? At the time of the death of her father Joseph, when in fact Jesus returned to see her for the first time "as a stranger," Ruth asked, this time more within herself, "If He healed, why did He let Father die? If He is such as so many proclaim, *why* hath He been so long away? *Why* does He continue to go here, there? Why do those that are in authority appear against Him?" (no. 1158–9).

References in the Cayce readings to James, the younger brother of Jesus and the older brother of Ruth, are relatively few and sparse in content. He is, however, identified as the one who "became as the head of what is termed the church" (no. 1158–5; compare Acts 15:12–21; Gal. 1:19; 2:9, 12). A few references are also made to Jude, the youngest brother in the family, as that he came to have faith in "the Master as the Master of the entity" for the first time about a year and a half after the death of Jesus (no. 137–64). He was then only nineteen years old. The readings also state that the short book in the New Testament attributed to Jude was in fact composed by him, evidently when he "wrote much in confinement at that place now called Achaia [Greece]" (no. 137–121).

Part II

THE PUBLIC MINISTRY

6
THE BEGINNINGS

THE PUBLIC MINISTRY of Jesus began in one sense with the events immediately preceding its public inauguration, namely, with his baptism in the river Jordan at the hands of his cousin John, and his subsequent experience of temptations in the wilderness (compare Mark 1:1–13; Matt. 3:1–4:11). That Jesus came to John to be baptized by him would seem to indicate his choice of John as the most authentic link with the prophetic past of Israel. And Jesus evidently believed that submission to the baptismal form of repentance taught and offered by John was the most appropriate way to begin his own prophetic mission.

The Edgar Cayce readings, however, enhance our understanding of these events. They have much to say about John, as the "kinsman who had been spoken of and held in awe, his mother having been a chosen vessel by the priests of the Essenes, and he, John, being the lineal descendant of the high priests of the Jews" (no. 1158–4; compare Luke 1:5). The last item refers to the priestly lineage of John's father, Zechariah.

John is further described as "one that had renounced his position as a priest that might serve in the temple, to become an outcast and a teacher in the wilderness" (no. 1158–4). Now the readings identify John's father with the "Zechariah the son of Barachiah" briefly mentioned in the Gospel of

Matthew by Jesus himself as having been wantonly "murdered between the sanctuary and the altar" (Matt. 23:35). (In the Old Testament Zechariah the son of Barechiah (sic) is the prophet of that name who began his prophetic career in 520 B.C., the second year of the reign of the Persian king Darius (Zech. 1:1). The prophet Zechariah who is described as having been stoned to death in the temple by command of King Joash of Judah is cited as the son of Jehoida (2 Chron. 24:21); his death occurred perhaps shortly after 805 B.C. In Matthew, therefore, the reference is most likely to a person other than either of these two.) The readings also affirm that the reason for his murder was the public proclamation of his religious experience and subsequent committal to the Essene cause (compare Luke 1:8–23, 57–80).

Thus it would appear at least in part the result of deep personal feelings that John renounced his expected priestly role, for his own father, who, as we read in Luke, was a priest of "the division of Abijah" and therefore of the Aaronic line, had been so ruthlessly treated by the religious establishment. For Jesus to initiate his public ministry by baptism at the hands of this John is therefore also indicative symbolically of the direction of his preferences in the religious spectrum of Israel in his time. This action must have been seen by the religious establishment—the high priestly families, the Sadduccees, the Pharisees—as indicating that the main direction of Jesus' ministry could be, from their point of view, sectarian or even heterodox.

The above, however, is not to say that the Cayce readings affirm either the teachings or the lifestyle of Jesus to be completely in conformity with those of John. John taught and practiced an extreme mode of physical abstinence for the sake of purification of the body. In contrast Jesus allowed freedom "in those things that to some became questioned," yet in such a way as to keep "the body for those purposes alone where unto He had called same to be beautiful in its relationships" (no. 609–1; compare Mark 1:6; 2:18–22; Matt. 11:18–19). As we have already noted, the readings state that "John was more the Essene than Jesus. For Jesus held rather to the spirit of the law, and John to the letter of same" (no. 2067–11).

The Edgar Cayce readings, like the insights of Rudolf Steiner, perceive Jesus' experience of baptism as having critical importance for his public ministry in the deepest spiritual sense. We read that Jesus at this time "received those acknowledgments of the Father that He was the one who could, *would,* through those activities, become the Savior of man" (no. 262–29, A-3; compare Mark 1:9–10). That is, Jesus became aware at this time in a notable way that indeed God the Father had made him his primary instrument for the salvation (reconciliation, restoration, complete transformation) of all humanity. Hearing the words "in whom I am well pleased" at the time of his baptism, and "This is my Son; hear ye Him" later on the occasion of his transfiguration, became for Jesus, according to the readings, signal steps in the development of his awareness of both his mission and his relationship with the Father (no. 262–29, A-3; compare Mark 1:11;9:7).

The readings state that Jesus' baptism was also the fulfillment or completion of his initiation (no. 2067–7). From there he went out into the wilderness to undergo what the readings call "the tests in the wilderness" (no. 1158–4). The purpose, however, of this latter activity is also described as having been "to meet that which had been His undoing in the beginning" (no. 2067–7). This is, we note again, reference to Jesus' need to recapitulate, as the second Adam and with full victory, the earlier experience of temptation and fall as the first Adam (compare 1 Cor. 15:20–22).

The readings then speak of Jesus' return from these experiences to the city of Capernaum in Galilee (no. 1158–4; compare Luke 4:14–15; Mark 1:21). The fourth chapter of Luke states that Jesus' return from the Judean wilderness was to Galilee, where he taught "in their synagogues." Jesus is then described by Luke as going to Nazareth, "where he had been brought up." The content of his sermon in the synagogue in Nazareth is given, together with the angry response of many of his hearers (Luke 4:16–30). Luke then writes of Jesus' going (again?) to Capernaum, where he preached and healed on the sabbath and where he healed Peter's mother-in-law in Peter's house (Luke 4:31–41). In Mark 1:21 the first sentence cited of Jesus' preaching in a synagogue is in Capernaum.

In the readings Jesus' first preaching in a synagogue in Capernaum is described as relating "to the prophecies of Isaiah, Jeremiah, and the teachings of the lesser prophets, and as to how they applied in the experiences of that day" (no. 1158–4). This statement helps us to understand the strong and consistent emphasis of the Cayce readings upon the application of truth to daily life as being a central aspect of Jesus' teaching and practice. The result of this first preaching after the return from the wilderness is given as that "a tumult was raised owing to the utterances of that new teacher" (no. 1158–4).

7

THE EARLY MIRACLES

THE CAYCE READINGS state that while "the first of
the outward miracles of healing" (no. 3175–1; compare
Mark 1:29–31) was the healing of Peter's mother-in-law, the
first recorded miracle was that of turning water into wine in
Cana of Galilee, which is said to be "nigh unto Capernaum"
(no. 5749–16; compare John 2:1–12). This is one of a number of instances where the Cayce materials prefer the order
of events in the public ministry of Jesus as given in the
Gospel of John. The miracle at Cana—the readings do not
hesitate to denote either this event or the physical healings
with the term "miracles"—is said to have occurred "soon
after the return of the Master from the Jordan, and His dwelling by the sea, His conversation with Peter—after Andrew
had told Peter of the happenings at the Jordan; and there was
the wedding in Cana of Galilee" (no. 5749–15; compare
John 1:35–42).

The readings suggestively put this event in the context of
various questionings of Jesus by his mother, "with her son
returning as a man starting upon his mission" (no. 5749–
15). Mary had continued to reflect upon the events surrounding Jesus' birth—the pronouncement of the angel Gabriel,
the strange experiences incident to her visit with Elizabeth
(compare Luke 1:26–56)—and the later unusual events in
Egypt and on the return to Palestine (compare Matt. 2:13–

23). "This might be called a first period of test. For, had He not just ten days ago sent Satan away, and received ministry from the angels?" (no. 5749–15).

Evidently Mary had already heard of these matters through others, and her first meeting with her son after his temptation experience was on this day of the wedding feast at Cana. Jesus' primary purpose in coming to Cana was evidently to speak with his mother, who had this "natural questioning of the mother-love for the purposes; this son—strange in many ways—had chosen, by dwelling in the wilderness for the forty days, and then [by] the returning to the lowly peoples, the fishermen" (no. 5749–15; compare Luke 5:1–11), to fulfill his calling in ways that were still puzzling to her.

Another reading describes the miracle at Cana in poetic language as "when water saw its Master, blushed, and became wine even by activity! Remember, only as it was poured out would it become wine" (no. 3361–1). Here, too, as so often in the Cayce readings, eloquent statement of the way of Jesus is turned into teaching of that way as pattern for our own daily life. The larger meaning of the event at Cana, however, is suggested by the statement in another reading that refers to "the blessings of having the Master present at the wedding." This reading goes on to speak of the divine significance of human marriage, which is described as properly involving "the union of hearts and minds and bodies. . . ." The reading concludes by saying, in direct address to the person for whom it was given, "Know, in thine heart of hearts, as bodies and minds are drawn together, these are not purposeless but purposeful, that the glory of God may be made manifest" (no. 2946–3).

MEETINGS WITH INDIVIDUALS

The next event in the public ministry of Jesus given some prominence in the Cayce readings is his healing the fever of the mother of Simon Peter's wife (compare Mark 1:29–31).

This event is signaled as "one of the few instances where healings were performed among His own people, among His own kindred" (no. 5749–16). These words seem to refer to Jesus' performing healings only in a very limited way within his own extended family.

It may be well to mention at this point what the readings say about Martha, cited as the much younger sister of Peter's mother-in-law. This Martha, who is to be distinguished from Martha the sister of Mary and Lazarus (compare Luke 10: 38–41; John 11:1–44), married Nicodemus, the distinguished Pharisee and member of the ruling Jewish council called the Sanhedrin. He is described in a famous passage in the Gospel of John as coming to Jesus secretly by night and receiving teaching noteworthy for both him and all humanity (John 3: 1–21). "Though Martha was an Essene, Nicodemus never accepted completely the tenets or teachings of the Essene group. These were a part of the principles and applications of Martha" (no. 3175–3).

This, then, was the particular context of activities and developments within which "Nicodemus went to the Master by night, and there became those discussions in the home; for Nicodemus and Martha there began the communion as man and wife rather than man and his chattel or his servant. They were more on a basis of equality" (no. 3175–3). Here, as elsewhere in the Cayce readings, we find information specifically indicating how Jesus and his teaching worked to elevate the status of women and to effect the purification and ennoblement of relationships within the family.

This Martha is said to have been "one particularly honored even by the Master" (no. 3175–3). She came to be one of the leaders among the early disciples, and she was present at Jesus' crucifixion as "one of those upon the right hand of Mary, the mother of Jesus" (compare Mark 15:40–41). On the festival of Pentecost, when the Holy Spirit was signally manifested, she was "among those who heard all of the various places announce their hearing Peter in their own tongue" (compare Acts 2:1–42). Martha "later was among those who aided Stephen and Philip, as well as others of the various lands'' (compare Acts 6–8).

She became an advisor and teacher as well as helper, especially to the younger ministers and workers in the early church. Her ''home became more and more a place of refuge and help for all of the young of the church,'' and apparently her two sons and one daughter became ministers in the church in Antioch of Syria. This daughter, we read, was later wed to Silas, one of the missionary colleagues of the Apostle Paul. Martha herself ''lived to be an elderly person, something like seventy-nine years of age in the experience, and was not among those ever beaten or placed in jail'' (no. 3175–3), although she experienced persecution in other forms.

We find several references in the Cayce readings to the meeting of Jesus with a Samaritan woman by the well of Jacob, as described in the famous passage in the Gospel of John (4:1–42). Incidentally, we learn from a reading that there were also Samaritans who were ''from the land of the Galileans'' (no. 5328–1). That is, as one would normally expect from the relative mobility of society in that time and place, those of the Samaritan faith were not confined to the geographical limits of Samaria proper. The readings stress the individual and then the larger consequences of the meeting of the Master with this woman by contrasting the quality of her life before and after the encounter.

For as the entity had wielded its influence for that which brought those of distorted emotions and ideas in the minds of individuals during that period, so, with the awakening of the water of life springing anew in the hearts and souls of those that made Him as the ideal, did the entity bring into the minds, hearts, and souls of those first of its own household, then of the multitudes, then of the greater masses, that of the *beauty of life* in Him, of the glories of the Father in Him, as may be manifested in the lives of individuals

who have Him as their ideals, whether pertaining to
the secular things of life or otherwise—for the crust of
bread glorified by Him feeds in the physical body those
things that bring glories in the hearts and minds of
individuals, where the sumptuous board of those that
wander far away must bring dimness of eye, solemn-
ness of feeling, want and desire in the hearts of those
that follow such. . . . (no. 451–2)

Some readers may recall in this context the rather long-
standing controversy (especially among Protestant Christians
in North America and elsewhere) as to whether the primary
significance of the person and work of Jesus lies in his being
ideal or in being savior. On this issue the Cayce readings
consistently maintain a "both and" position. That is, Jesus
is both ideal and savior, both the example for all persons and
the redeemer of all.

We read also that members of the immediate family of
this Samaritan woman later "became messengers and under-
standers of that being taught" (no. 451–2). It is said of her
sister that reflection coupled "with the faith that was implanted by this meeting—brought peace, joy, understanding,
and the ability to suffer, even in silence, whether in physical,
in mental, or the material things of life" (no. 428–4). This
sister is said to have given much to others in that period,
"bringing peace to her own household, quietude to those
disturbed in body and mind" (no. 428–2).

The Cayce readings tell of another person who "came in
close contact with the Master when the Master spoke to the
woman at the well and [to] many of those in the city who
came out to see Him" (no. 1552–1). This person, "though
then young in years . . . was impressed . . . by the gentleness
and kindness of the disciples, especially the Master" (no.
1552–1). We learn in the same context that "as His teachings
had advanced" (no. 1552–1), the Samaritans who accepted
them came to participate more and more in the great festivals
in Jerusalem, evidently effecting a significant degree of rec-

onciliation between Jew and Samaritan during the lifetime of Jesus.

An even stronger statement of the larger effects of Jesus' meeting with the Samaritan woman is given in another reading, where reference is made to "that city which later turned a great deal of its activity because of the visit of the Master to the woman at the well" (no. 1592–1). This was the visit "of the man of Galilee, the man who walked among His fellow man that others might be shown the way for the more perfect understanding" (no. 379–3), the one who also "came as the lamb to the world" (no. 933–1). This is he who also said, "Not of myself . . . but [from] the Father that worketh in and through me do I bring thee health, do I bring thee hope, do I bring thee the living water" (no. 1152–4; compare John 4:10–14; 5:19; 14:10). The Cayce readings sum up the quality of the daily life of Jesus with the sentence, "Love in its essence is manifested in every word, act, thought, and experience of the body" (no. 262–25).

Among the reports of activities in the early public ministry of Jesus we find various references, mostly fragmentary, to the first disciples. Sometimes we have telling vignettes of the Master's followers, as when "the staid Andrew" is contrasted with "the boisterous Peter" (no. 4016–1). A member of the seventy sent out by Jesus on a missionary journey within Israel found that "he argued with Peter and reasoned with Andrew" (no. 4016–1).

JESUS' PHYSICAL APPEARANCE

Jesus' physical appearance is described briefly in at least two of the Cayce readings, a noteworthy contribution since neither the New Testament nor other early Christian literature gives us any hints of this kind. One reading speaks of Jesus' profile as being neither distinctively Semitic nor Aryan. His appearance, we learn, was "clear, clean, ruddy, hair almost like that of David, golden brown, yellow-red, but blue eyes [described in reading no. 5749–1 as being "blue or steel-gray"] which were piercing; and the beard, not cut, but kept in the proportion of the face, and the head was almost perfect" (no. 5354–1). In a reading requested for an account of the Lord's Supper (which we shall consider in more detail later) Cayce gave the following description of the physical appearance of Jesus: "The Master's hair is 'most red, inclined to be curly in portions, yet not feminine or weak—*strong*, with heavy, piercing eyes that are blue or steel-gray. His weight would be at least a hundred and seventy pounds, long tapering fingers, nails well kept. Long nail, though, on the left little finger" (no. 5749–1).

Some readers may reflect upon reading this description that it sounds like the product of a skillfully imaginative historical novelist. Indeed it does; but it is also true that the description, even as imaginative literature, seems in keeping with the probabilities of the historical situation to the extent that we know it. According to the Cayce readings, then, this was the way Jesus appeared to "those throngs that gathered at times for the interpreting of the new teachings, and the watching of their application in the experience of Him—who gave such hope to the world" (no. 3360–1).

Here we read that the crowds were watching to see how Jesus practiced what he preached. This matter of application, however, is an issue of fundamental importance in the Cayce readings' perception of Jesus' own activity as of the content of his teachings. We may note that Jesus' teaching is said to have dealt primarily with principles rather than individual problem cases—although he never hesitated to receive individuals. One brief summation of the larger meaning of the person and work of Jesus the Christ is "that in Him is the life and the light, and that His whole command is *sincerity and love*" (no. 2015–3; compare John 15:12). But when a person asked the sleeping Cayce, "How may I be most useful to Jesus Christ?" the answer was: "In applying principles . . . in thy daily life, in dealing with thy fellow men" (no. 1646–2).

Another reading refers to the story in the Gospel of Luke of the ten lepers who came to ask Jesus for healing. They were all healed, but only one came back to express his thanks (Luke 17:11–19). The reading adds that one of the nine who did not return to give thanks is said to have "gained and lost through that experience," a frequent expression in the Cayce readings. He gained in awareness but "lost in not making a practical application of same in its experience among its fellow men, not bearing witness to those assurances, those experiences, in its activity" (no. 2181–1).

TRAVELS IN THE EARLY MINISTRY

The Cayce readings make several references to Jesus' traveling in the early portion of his public ministry, not only in the northern sections of Jewish Palestine but also for "the edifying of the peoples in the outer areas of Palestine" (no. 3640–1). Some people in these areas experienced and "ever gave thanks for the manner in which the Master indicated His interest in others, their sorrows, their joys, their uprisings, their littleness, and their abilities to appreciate" (no. 3640–1). In this spirit and manner the "Prince of Peace entered into [the country of the Gadarenes—or Gerasenes]" (no. 2481–1; compare Mark 5:1–20; Matt. 8:28–34), and journeyed into the territories of Tyre and Sidon, "the upmost coast of the land" (no. 513–1; compare Mark 7:24–31).

Some came from long distances, that is, from outside Jewish Palestine, "hearing of the healings and of the Master's activities through portions of the land" (no. 3640–1; compare Matt. 4:24–25; Mark 3:7–8; Luke 6:17). Some "brought their loved ones to the Master for healing" and found that, "He supplied that as would bring happiness and joy; not gratification but contentment and peace to the hearts and souls of those that sought to know His biddings" (no. 3216–1).

Jesus, "The Teacher of teachers, the Lord of lords, the

Brother of man" (no. 2035–1), he who "was . . . is the life, the light in this material world . . ." also sojourned in what is called "the land of the Saracens" (no. 2661–1). The Saracens, a term rarely used in contemporary English, is derived from a late Greek word that came to designate Arabs in general and finally all Muslim subjects of the caliphate. More narrowly, however, the name Saracen appears to have been used for a nomadic people of Semitic stock and language living in the deserts between Syria and the Arabian peninsula. The terminology of the Cayce readings seems to be in accord with this narrower geographical usage and indicates a specific area outside Jewish Palestine where Jesus taught and healed.

THE MISSION OF THE SEVENTY

There are several references in the Cayce readings to the mission of the seventy who, according to the witness of the Gospel of Luke, were sent out by Jesus on a teaching-healing mission in preparation for his own later arrival at various places (Luke 10: 1–12; compare 9: 1–2, 51–52). We learn from Cayce how "the Master blessed the seventy that were to go abroad and teach and minister to others and preach repentance, that the day of the Lord was at hand" (no. 1529–1).

As a further expression of this "realized eschatology," another reading states that members of the seventy were "able, by the blessing of the Master, to heal physically and mentally" (no. 5328–1). We read also of "each individual being commissioned by the Master, Jesus Himself" (no. 3395–3). Elsewhere we are told that "those that had become the leaders and the teachers . . . were tested, trained, taught by Him" (no. 857–1). One sentence describes their being "sent as emissaries through the land to proclaim periods in which there would be activity of the Master as combined with the teachings and ministering of many of the apostles" (no. 2285–1). We learn in another reading that the apostles were at first called only disciples. The term "apostles" evidently was given later as some of the disciples came to be assigned specifically missionary tasks (no. 2459–1). It would seem, therefore, that the term "disciples," or learners of God through Jesus, was the principal designation of his followers.

We read also that the seventy were sent out on at least two different occasions, "during the Galilean as well as the Judean ministry" (no. 622–4; see also no. 3347–1). The Cayce readings suggest that the mission of the seventy is one that should be repeated again and again by the followers of Jesus also in our present day. The nature of that mission is

> to bring into the hearts of men again and again *hope*, encouragement; and to *sow* again and again the seeds that bear the fruits of the Spirit—patience, gentleness, kindness, brotherly love, long-suffering! For against such there is no law [compare Gal. 5:22–23].
>
> For it is the law that as ye sow, so shall ye reap [compare Gal. 6:7]. And ye are the sower; but leave what may be the results to thy Father!
>
> For He alone may increase. For unless the souls be quickened by the precept and the example, and the Father calleth, how can they know Him? (no. 1529–1)

The Cayce readings frequently use the word "law" to denote the complete integrity and essential regularity of God's way in the universe, so that the processes of nature and the course of human history are seen as under God's ultimate control even as human beings are endowed with freedom of the will—within limits. The readings sometimes also use the term "law" in the sense of the law of God (Torah) as believed and practiced in the Jewish tradition. With reference to this latter meaning, the readings emphasize that Jesus' posture was selective but constructive; he focused on the essence of this (Jewish) law, he did not abolish it.

With reference to the much debated question of divine judgment based on the law, we find in the Cayce readings that "He [Jesus] condemned not." But we also learn that he said more than once that, "Indeed, offenses must come, but woe unto them by whom they come" (no. 2031–1; compare Matt. 18:7). By this conjunction of apparently contradictory themes, the readings, here, as elsewhere, insist that Jesus never condemned anyone in the sense of closing off his or her future, but at the same time he made clear that the law of sowing and reaping, of cause and effect, continues to operate—in the moral and spiritual as well as in the physical realms of the universe. This is therefore to say that the operation of the casual law is open-ended, that the transcendent power of God's mercy takes precedence over all other laws and functions so as to enable those who would cooperate with him to be liberated, to cope and ultimately to overcome all experiences of separation and failure (sin).

The Cayce statement of the nature of the mission of Jesus' followers seems superbly appropriate to any time or place, applicable to both clergy and laity. The missioners are to teach and to be examples, all in the larger context of the Father's continued working (compare John 5:17). The Cayce readings emphasize that Jesus himself both taught and exemplified, telling us of "that truth which He so thoroughly exemplified in the experiences of man: namely, to love the Lord thy God with all thy heart, thy mind, thy body, and thy neighbor as thyself—which is the whole law" (no. 2031–1; compare Mark 12:28–31).

This same reading goes on to say that an appropriate contemporary reenactment of the activity of the seventy would be to "keep this experience [as one of the seventy] in such manners that day by day—not so much by proclamation of thyself, but by thy gentleness, by thy kindness, by thy tenderness of words, of hope, of cheer, of that ever giving of creative forces in their experiences—others may be led to know that ye walk and talk with Him."

INTIMATIONS OF THE LORD'S SUPPER

The Cayce readings state that it was after the return of the seventy from their missionary activity that Jesus taught what the Gospel of John identifies as an offense-giving statement, namely, that persons "must eat of the body and drink of the blood if they are to know the Lord" (compare John 6:35–71). The person for whom this reading was given was told that he himself had been present at that time and place and

> like many others the entity went away, but kept in touch with the activities; and with the day of Pentecost, when many were turned, the entity again became one of those associated with organized work. For then the entity understood, when there had been explained how on the night He was betrayed He took bread and broke it saying, "This is my body," and with the cup, "This is my blood." (no. 5328–1; compare Mark 14: 22–24)

Another person was also said to have been "among those who could not interpret upon the return: 'Except ye eat of my body, ye have no part in me'" (no. 4016–1; compare John 6:53). The explanation was then given: "Literal, it becomes disturbing. Mentally and in a spiritual sense, it may be interpreted."

The nature of what in fact is involved in the Lord's Supper as a sacrament of the church and reality of spiritual communion is further explained in the Cayce readings as in a sense including both physical and spiritual dimensions.

> For the Christ, as manifested in Jesus, was the first, is the foremost [compare John 1:1–2, 15], is the essence of both bread and of wine. For that element which is life-giving physically of bread, or that giveth strength to wine, is the source of life itself. Thus in partaking, one does literally partake of the body and of the blood in that communion. (no. 5328–1)

This statement seems to mean that the "life-giving" element in bread or wine—presumably any kind of bread or wine, whether sacramentally consecrated or not—is its essence, is also the source of life itself and is to be identified with the Universal Christ, the Second Person of the Trinity, who was manifested in Jesus of Nazareth. Such would evidently mean that the "Real Presence" is not confined to sacramentally consecrated bread and wine but may be experienced in association with any and all "life-giving" things.

We should add, however, that the statement is not to be understood pantheistically, as if all is God without distinction. Such is not the teaching of the Cayce readings, wherein, for example, both individual consciousness and freedom of will in human beings are consistently affirmed. The readings do repeatedly speak of a certain solidarity in and of all life, but such as to allow meaningfully working distinctions of consciousness that constitute and enable human freedom. Thus we read

> It should be understood that Life is One, that each soul, each entity is a part of the Whole, able, and capable of being one with the Source, or the Universal Power, God, yet capable of being individual, independent entities in their own selves. As He has given, to those whom He calls does He give the power to become the sons of God. (no. 294-155; compare John 1:12–13)

Apparently, in the mystery of the relationship of human beings as persons to God, their Maker and Sustainer, there are elements of both dependence and freedom. But for that relationship to attain its proper form or destiny, the dialogic reciprocity of divine call and human response, of particular appeal and willing cooperation, is necessary. "*Open* then thy heart, thy consciousness, for He would tarry with thee!" (no. 5755–1).

Both the fact of human freedom and possible variations of

the consequences of the fact are frequently affirmed in the readings. Thus: "we are joint heirs with that Universal Force we call God—if we seek to do His biddings. If our purposes are not in keeping with that Creative Force, or God, then we may be a hindrance" (no. 5755–2). We read: "Only they that seek shall find!" (no. 5755–1). Another reading puts it thus: "He comes not unbidden, but as ye seek ye find; as ye knock it is opened. As ye live the life is the awareness of His closeness, of His presence, thine" (no. 5749–10; compare Matt. 7:7–8).

Therefore the partaking of the elements of bread and wine in the sacrament of the Lord's Supper is indeed a participation in the Source of life itself, in the Christ of the Godhead. But for this participation to have spiritual and moral significance—saving, ethically transforming power—questing, requesting human aspiration for the Godhead (one aspect of this aspiration may of course properly be called faith) is necessary.

On other occasions, however, the Cayce readings prefer to speak of the human role as response to divine initiative, as in the following: "Know that He stands at the door of thy heart and thy mind and knocks, and would enter and sup with thee! If ye will but invite Him!" (no. 1641–1; compare Rev. 3:20). There are frequent references in the Cayce readings to the famous passage of Revelation 3:20 and its beautiful imagery denotive of divine call and human response. Thus we read: "He that would know his own way, his own relationships to Creative Forces or God, may seek through the promises in Him, as set in Jesus of Nazareth—He passeth by! Will ye have Him enter and sup with thee?" (no. 5755–1).

8

THE MAJOR MIRACLES

IN THE CASE of Jesus' healings of the sick and infirm, a distinction is sometimes made in the Cayce readings between the physical and the moral-spiritual aspects of the process. Thus in the case of the "leper at the gate" who was healed by Jesus (compare Mark 1:40–45), the statement is made that "the entity was *healed* (physical), made clean (moral) . . . [that he might] gain the better understanding of self, through those lessons taught by that Teacher" (no. 2482–1).

The readings indicate in a number of cases that moral wrong or sin may be the primary cause of physical illness. In one of the 5749 series of readings, we find a discussion of Jesus' healing the paralytic who was brought to Jesus' home in Capernaum and let down by his friends before Jesus by opening a hole in the roof (compare Mark 2:1–12). Cayce notes that this was one of many of Jesus' healings that were instantaneous, but as in the biblical account, the reading states that Jesus initiated the healing process by saying to the paralytic, "Son, thy sins be forgiven thee."

When the questionings came (as He knew they would), He answered, "Which is it easier to say, thy sins be forgiven thee, or arise, take up thy bed and go into thine house?" *Immediately* the man arose, took up his bed and *went* into his house! Here we find that it was

not by the command, but by His own personage. For
the question was not as to whether He healed but as
to whether He had the power to forgive sin! The rec-
ognition was that sin had caused the physical distur-
bance. (no. 5749–16)

Several meanings can be drawn from this passage, one
being that Jesus addressed the interior state of the man as
his prior need. Another aspect of the interpretation given by
Cayce is that while the physical healing was instantaneous
and indeed "miraculous," the entire event was not effected
by mere pronouncement. Rather, it particularly involved the
influence of Jesus' person upon the man, to the end that he
responded with both faith and obedience, cooperating fully
in the process of healing. The importance of this kind of
human response to divine initiative is indicated in another
reading, "He that is called to service must indeed obey" (no.
294–155).

In another reading Cayce was asked to "explain why the
Master in many cases forgave sin in healing individuals."
The answer given was, "Sins are of commission and omis-
sion. Sins of commission were forgiven, while sins of omis-
sion were called to mind—even by the Master" (281–2). (A
helpful discussion of the relationship between healing and
the forgiveness of sins in the ministry of Jesus is given by
the German biblical scholar Otto Betz in *What Do We Know
About Jesus.*)

Several references are made in the readings to Jesus' restoration to life of a widow's son at a town called Nain (compare Luke 7:11–17), "when the widow of Nain was stopped
by the Master" (5248–1). Elsewhere we read that "the entity
received back alive the son—as they walked from Nain at
those periods of His ministry there" (no. 601–2), and "the
son was delivered again to the mother" (no. 2454–3).

Reference is also made to a person who was "among those
groups chosen as companions upon many of the missions
which the Master took." This person is said to have been

present at the time of Jesus' stilling of a storm, for "the entity saw that experience of the wind, of the storm—the elements, the thunder, the lightning obey the voice of the Master." In this same context we find Jesus spoken of in the most exalted terms as "Him, who is the God of the storm, God of peace, God of the wind, God of the rain, yea, the Lord of the earth, of whom the disciples said, 'what manner of man is this, that even the wind and the rain, the sea and the elements obey His voice" (no. 5276–1; compare Mark 4:35–41).

Brief references are made in the readings to the biblical accounts of the casting out of demons from two men of the country of the Gadarenes, an area that we have already noted as being outside Jewish Palestine (compare Matt. 8:28–34). This incident is cited as another instance when Jesus came to those "in the outer coasts of the land" (no. 1934–1). One reading describes the event as that "when the influences were driven from the man in the Gadarene land" (1616–1). Here we find reference to the exorcism of but one man, as in the Marcan version in the New Testament (Mark 5:1–20). The readings taken together, however, seem to harmonize the differing Matthean and Marcan versions by suggesting that while there were two afflicted men who were from the tombs, only one could be described as having been "possessed" (1934–1; 1616–1).

This event of exorcism, according to one reading, became the occasion for Jesus to teach with special emphasis that God is to be known and addressed as "Father God" (no. 1616–1). Another reading indicates that the event had profound effects also upon others than those healed, as in the case of one who "learned gentleness, kindness, patience—as was shown in the gentle manner in which all were answered who raised their voice in criticism of the activities of that particular experience" (no. 1934–1).

The criticism mentioned here refers of course to the scriptural accounts of how the demons driven out by Jesus were allowed to enter into a herd of swine grazing nearby, which in turn became so agitated that they rushed down a steep bank and were drowned in the sea (of Galilee). This loss of property evidently stirred up the whole community and they asked Jesus to leave their area (compare Matt. 8:34; Mark 5:17; Luke 8:37).

Several references are made in the readings to Jesus' calling back from the dead the daughter of a man named Jairus, one of the rulers of a local synagogue in Galilee (compare Mark 5:21–43). In one reading the event is spoken of as that which happened to the ''one whom the Master called again from the deep sleep—Jairus's daughter'' (no. 559–7). In another it is said that her parents ''had their loved one given again to them as a *living* example of His indeed being the resurrection'' (no. 1968–4). In yet another the mother is addressed and told how she was able to see ''in body the love in the flesh presented to thy arms, by the love of the Son of the Father God!'' (no. 1968–1).

In this same reading, while reference is also made to ''the patience of the man of Galilee,'' we are told ''how stern He might be when He put the entity out of the room, as well as those of the household, because of doubt'' (compare Mark 5:40). The lesson to be gained from that experience was and is, we are told, to put ''the whole trust in the faith of Him that is the way and light and truth and understanding!'' And again, with reference to the nature and scope of Jesus' healing, this reading states that ''His presence [was] to heal body, mind and soul.'' We are also told here of Jesus' ''love for man, of His filling the whole life purpose of man'' (no. 1968–1).

A later reading for the same person refers again to the healing of Jairus's daughter and speaks of ''the blessings to be had materially and mentally from the embracing of those principles and tenets of the Teacher'' (no. 1968–4). This point of the practicality of Jesus' teaching is correlate to the frequent statement in the Cayce readings that Jesus was concerned for every aspect of human life and acted, as well as taught, accordingly. This same reading indicates that Jairus had previously been influenced by the teachings of both John the Baptizer and Jesus. One consequence of such openness was that Jairus was commended by the Master because he had shown an "unusual interest of man for his mate, and for the offspring, for the period of time." This attitude and practice of Jairus also brought "wonderment from his associates or companions in his office" (no. 1968-4).

The call of Jairus' daughter back to life on earth was a call "back to service in that experience" (no. 421-5). She herself was addressed, we are told, in the following fashion: "Awake, my daughter, to the abilities of thyself through the might of the God Force within thee" (no. 1246-2; compare Mark 5:41). "The man of might and power through Galilee" said to her, "Arise and minister" (no. 1246-2). She, like others, became "a changed person in those days because of the happenings there" (no. 3307-1).

Jesus' healing of the woman who had had a flow of blood for twelve years is an incident mentioned in the gospel accounts in temporal connection with the raising of Jairus's daughter (Mark 5:24-34 and parallels).

A Cayce reading describes the woman in some detail as "a very thin or pale individual, with very dark eyes and hair—and a robe of gray and purple, or the bands about same, purple while the robe would be in a lighter gray." She is seen as "kneeling upon one knee and reaching for the hem of the Master's robes—and He turned as to the left to encounter the figure kneeling, see?" (no. 585-10). This same reading also adds further descriptive data with regard to Jesus himself. He is pictured as "the Master with the grey robe, the beard scant, the hair—not red nor yet golden, but as of reddish golden—blessing or healing the woman with the issue."

FEEDING THE MULTITUDES

The miracles of Jesus' feeding large multitudes with a few loaves of bread and fishes are referred to a number of times in the Cayce readings, often in connection with the blessing of children. Like the New Testament accounts, the readings mention two different events, one the feeding of five thousand men, the second four thousand persons (compare Mark 6:30–44; 8:1–10 and parallels). (In the Gospel of Matthew the numbers cited, five thousand and four thousand, are followed in each case by the additional phrase, "besides women and children" [Matt. 14:21; 15:38]. Luke mentions only the feeding of the five thousand "men" [Luke 9:14]. The Cayce reading that refers to feeding four thousand is no. 3183–1.)

The event of feeding the five thousand in particular is singled out as an occasion when the Master blessed many, notably the young persons present. One reading, addressed to a woman who is said to have been among the children blessed on "that day when the five thousand were fed," tells how as a result of that experience "the whole reliance upon the faith in those promises made manifest in Him held the entity to an experience of helpfulness to others." The reading goes on to tell this person, "He blessed thee in the flesh. He will bless thee again, if thou holdest to that purpose, putting away strife, jealousy, malice, condemnation. Condemn not, if ye would not be condemned" (no. 1614–2; compare Matt. 7:1–2).

The readings consistently affirm the events as historical and physical fact, and offer a number of significant insights and lessons. One reading states that the entity who requested the reading had participated in the event and in particular had learned patience from that and related experiences. "For He did not lose patience with His disciples when they said, 'Should we go away to buy bread to feed this mob?' " Giving concrete expression to a theme often emphasized in the Cayce materials—the necessity of starting where one is and using what one has in hand—the reading quotes Jesus himself as saying to the disciples "What have we here? What have you here?" (compare Mark 6:38; 8:5). The account then goes on to say,

Did you ever hear this used to individuals? Try it! It is one of the most disturbing, yet one of the most quieting words which may be used, even to a mob. "What have we here?" And only a few loaves, a few fishes, yet in the hands of those who could realize, as ye may, "Of myself, I can do nothing, but through His power" [compare John 5:19], it may be multiplied into blessings. And remember, it can be multiplied in curses, also, if ye use not thy abilities aright. (no. 5089–2)

The Cayce readings therefore see the events of Jesus' feeding multitudes as activities that can be applied to a significant degree in the experience of all people; but at the same time they affirm a certain uniqueness. Thus the statement is made that "the thousands were fed as only the Master might feed, from the few loaves and fishes" (no. 5002–1). Another reading states that participation in the experience "brought the awareness of the unusualness and the divinity of the Master." In this instance another factor contributing to such awareness was "wonderments at His joining His disciples without means of transportation in the ship" (no. 2845–2; compare Mark 6:45–52). This latter event is referred to in another reading as "His walking on water and . . . His bidding Peter to come to Him" (no. 2829–1).

The readings interpret these events of Jesus' feeding multitudes as illustrative of general or cosmic principles of divine supply and increase of material as well as of other goods, principles applicable to the life of every person in any situation. In one reading, for instance, we are specifically told, "Do not count any condition lost. Rather make each the stepping stone to higher things, remembering that God does not allow us to be tempted beyond that we are able to bear and comprehend, if we will but make our wills one with His" (no. 900–44; compare 1 Cor. 10:13). Another reading says, "There are *always* opportunities! Opportunities are never withdrawn" (no. 333–6).

The Cayce readings, moreover, consistently affirm the reality of matter and see it as both good in itself and of God. Matter, however, while derivative of Spirit and created by the Most High, is perceived as in a sense subordinate to, even as it is expressive of the spiritual dimension: "Even as the Spirit moved, matter came into being" (no. 1770–2).

The high view of matter in the readings may be further perceived in the frequent anthropological analogy used to explain the nature and interrelationships of the Divine Trinity. In this analogy the God head is "explained" by equating the Father with the human body; the Christ, the Son, with the mind; the Holy Spirit, "through which all approach is made" (no. 1770–2), with the soul. We read that the Son as "the Mind became the Way, the Truth, the Light in materiality" (no. 1770–2).

The readings also affirm the principle and fact of what may be called secondary creation, for not all things in the material world are seen as the result of primary or original creation on the part of God the Father. Some things, such as "those things that corrupt good ground, those that corrupt the elements"—"elementals, and pests," for example—are perceived to be "the compounds" or consequential offspring of the beings or souls created in the primary divine creation (364–7). This worldview contemplates the possibility of human creativity, in common with the creativity of other beings spiritual in their essence, as potentially turning in directions either constructive or destructive. Such possibilities are the inevitable consequence of genuine freedom of the will, freedom frequently affirmed in the Cayce readings as our divine birthright.

This principle of secondary creation can of course be given the very widest interpretation and application in human social as well as individual life, in cultural, economic, and political spheres of activity. It means that human beings, who as souls are products of primary divine creation, are seen as capable of a wide range of truly creative activity. This activity is said to have its origin in the spiritual dimension, its direction or quality set in the mental, its manifestation in the material or physical. Thus, in a reading in which the context of reference is Jesus' feeding the five thousand, the statement is made, "But know, that which is material must have first had its inception in the spiritual—and has grown according to *mental* application" (no. 1743–1). In this same reading the proper religious application of this cosmic principle is given: "as the purpose of each soul is to be a channel through which that as held as its ideal is to be made manifest, and that the glory of God be kept first and foremost—then so live, so act as to be consistent in thy thoughts, thy acts, thy expressions. Not only in word but in deed. For being true to self will not make thee false to any." (This Shakespearean phrase [*Hamlet* I, 3, 78], which Cayce had evidently not read in his conscious life—although of course he may have heard it—occurs a number of times in the readings. Thus elsewhere we are told to "be true, to thine self—and it *cannot* be thou wilt be false to any" [no. 2135–1].) In all this one is not to forget the spiritual Source of "all power as may be manifested in the earth" (no. 1743–1).

Affirmation of divine supply of human needs is made frequently in the Cayce readings. He in whom we live and move and have our being "is the supply—whether it be material, the mental, the spiritual" (no. 1770–2; compare Acts 17:28). At one level of human experience the feeding of the five thousand was for "the supplying of physical needs to the material man" (no. 2549–1). But it was also the occasion on which "spiritual blessings came to many" (no. 2549–1). Indeed Jesus' "blessing and bringing abundance to others" were means of expressing his love and showing forth "the light of the life of the Christ" (no. 1770–2). These expressions of love and light and life are seen as manifestations of the heart and depth of the Father's compassion for the whole of his creation, for "why shouldn't a divine Father supply those worthy, and unworthy as well?" (no. 5398–1).

With regard, however, to this restatement of Jesus' teaching about the inclusive care of the Father for his entire creation—the Father who "makes his sun to rise on the evil

and on the good, and sends rain on the just and the unjust''
(Matt. 5:45)—the readings do not hesitate to warn against
human presumption toward God's so generous compassion
and care. Thus the very ''lad *from* whom Andrew obtained
the loaves and fishes to feed the five thousand''—this was a
truly important contribution, because however small in quantity and size, these were precisely the materials at hand that
could be used by the Master for multiplication—had gained
in his personal growth from ''that influence of increase, yet
not too great a gainer in the experience from the lesson there,
'Easy come, easy go' became too great an influence in that
particular sojourn'' (no. 1821–1). This person, addressed in
his current life expression, was warned in his reading that
participation in so great a blessing-event does not obviate the
fact ''that there are the needs each day for each soul to
choose aright, that there is today, as every day, set before
thee good and evil, life and death—Choose thou!'' (compare
Josh. 24:15).

Choices so made in the direction of the material or temporal ''as to blind self to the mental and spiritual needs''
bring appropriate consequences. ''For unless the purpose, the
ideal is founded in the spirituality, the increase, and the
growth—as ye experienced in seeing manifested to feed the
hordes that day—*cannot*, will not be a part of the experience!'' (no. 1821–1). As an example of Jesus' warning others—he never ''threatened''—we find in a reading what may
be considered one of his extracanonical sayings, ''As He
gave, 'Being forewarned, be forearmed, and allow not thine
house [thine self] to be broken up' '' (no. 1602–4; compare
Mark 3:20–27).

That is, having one's material needs supplied becomes a
positive part of the total self experience only as the material
is given its proper place and proportion in the hierarchy of
reality and value existent in both the cosmos as a whole and
the human self in particular. In this context of understanding
the following advice was offered. ''Then as He hath given,
and as ye heard so oft, 'The kingdom is within.' Turn ye

within, for there in the temple of thine own body is the temple of the living God, where He hath promised to meet thee, to commune with thee, and to give thee the supply of *all* that may be needed within thine experience'' (no. 1770–2; compare Luke 17:20–21; 1 Cor. 3:16; 6:19; 2 Cor. 6:16).

With regard to the affirmation frequently made in the Cayce readings that the kingdom of God is within the human self, we should also note the following: "It is *within* that there is the kingdom of heaven! The kingdom of *God* is without, but is manifested in how it is reacting upon thee— by the manner in which ye mete to thy associates day by day that concept of that light which arises within!" (no. 877–27; compare Luke 11:35). This distinction between the kingdom of heaven (the usage of the Gospel of Matthew) and the kingdom of God (the usage of Mark, Luke, John, Paul, and the early church in general) is evidently intended, here as elsewhere in the Cayce readings, to indicate that the proper realm of divine rule is both within and without, both internal and external, comprising the whole spectrum of human—and cosmic—existence. Incidentally, we may properly note that the correct translation of the Greek original of Luke 17:21 is "The kingdom of God is within you," and *not* the RSV-preferred "The kingdom of God is in the midst of you."

Thus the principle and process of divine supply are not to be regarded as functioning automatically or mechanically regardless of the kind or quality of human response. Proper human participation—materially, mentally, spiritually—is necessary for the process to keep rightly on its course. We read, "He that follows in *His* footsteps . . . [is] His, who said, 'Take my yoke upon you and learn of me.' And those that do such shall never—nor their seed—beg bread" (no. 457–3; compare Matt. 11:29; Ps. 37:25). There are also wrong ways to use divine supply: "there *is* the way that may seem right to a man, but the end thereof may be death" (no. 1770–2; compare Prov. 14:12). The right way is seen in advice given to a person who was said to have been present at Jesus' feeding of the multitude:

In the present walk ever closer with the Master. Let oft
the deeds of thy hands be multiplied by and through
Him, and not of thyself. For, these are the manners in
which ye may accomplish the most, letting that
power—which ye *saw* so well demonstrated—flow
through thee; by faith, yes, by works, yes; by the good
will that is a part of thy whole being—but ever the
power, the might in Him. (no. 3183–1)

Readers who have followed to some extent the attempts
of modern biblical scholarship to discern the source materials
of the New Testament gospel writers will be interested in
further statements in this reading. The person addressed is
said to have been among the early disciples of Jesus and to
have served as both teacher and writer, with the name Thaddeus (included, as Thaddaeus, in the lists of the twelve apostles given by Matthew and Mark—Matt. 10:3; Mark 3:18—
but not in Luke—Luke 6:12–16; Acts 1:13). This Thaddeus
is said to have taken notes that became "a part of the records
of Mark and Matthew, in Luke or John" and to have been
a personal acquaintance of the apostle John (no. 3183–1).
Reference is made in another reading to a woman named
Esther, who had "aided in compiling many of the letters
written by the writers of the Gospels in that particular period" (no. 3667–2). One more reading mentions a person
who was present in the Galilean town of Bethsaida during
Jesus' ministry there. This entity is said to have "aided others by the recording in its own terms, in its own language
[Aramaic?], the sayings and doings of the Master" and to
have "prompted Matthew to write his Gospel" (no. 3395–
2).

The properly nuanced human response to the generosity
of divine supply is suggested also in the sentence, "If thy
trust is put in the Lord of lords, ye may indeed revel in that
consciousness that 'The Lord will take care of many, as I do
His biddings' " (no. 5002–1). This statement of conditions
to the process and call to an ethically responsible relationship

with our Maker are given a large application in the following quotation from a reading that dealt precisely with the issue of the human role, the fact of stewardship, in obtaining needed divine supply:

Does mankind consider he is indeed his brother's keeper [compare Gen. 4:9]? This is the manner in which man may answer the question. There will be no want in bread for mankind when mankind eventually realizes he is indeed his brother's keeper. For the earth is the Lord's and the fullness thereof [Ps. 24:1], and the bounty in one land is lent to man to give his brother. Who is his brother? "Our Father" (we say)— then each of every land, of every color, of every creed is brother of those who seek the Father-God. (no. 5398-1)

This last reading, which was given on August 24, 1944— less than six months before Edgar Cayce's death on January 3, 1945—reveals to us in unforgettable language not only the principle of stewardship applied to human possession of material goods. It bases the whole process upon the prior principle of human solidarity in potential spiritual aspiration before the God of us all, solidarity that transcends all distinctions of place, race, or religious creeds. Everyone who aspires to the Most High—even as he or she perceives the Same—is my brother or sister.

One final point may be made with regard to Jesus' feeding the multitudes. As noted above, the event occurred within the larger context of the blessing of many, especially in this case the children and the young. A Cayce reading interprets the biblically recorded teaching of Jesus on the need for us all to become as little children in a way that seems helpful both to our understanding and to our practice. With reference to "the multiplying of things and experiences in the hand," a young woman who presumably had been one of the children blessed on that occasion long ago was advised, "Do not let these become a selfish thing. Let them be rather as He gave, when He blessed you—'Except ye become as little children, ye shall in no wise enter in'—unless ye are as forgiving, unless ye are as generous, unless ye are as dependent as little children . . .'' (no. 1523–1; see also no. 3395–2; compare Matt. 18:1–5). (It is noteworthy that this Cayce reading follows the text of the Gospel of Matthew more closely than that of Mark (9:33–37) or Luke (9:46–48).

Another Cayce reading describes

> how oft he used children, the young people, as the hope of the world, as to how each individual puts away those selfish desires which arise and becomes as little children, [or] one may never quite understand the simplicity of Christ's faith: Christ-like faith, Christ-like simplicity, Christlike forgiveness, Christ-like love, Christ-like helpfulness to others. (no. 1223–9)

Yet another reading gives us further aspects of Jesus' teaching on this theme:

> He taught His followers, His beloved disciples, that humbleness of heart, singleness or centralness of purpose, with the very expression of same as the child: that hurts must be forgiven, that neglect must be overlooked, that dissension must be of short duration, that such, and of such, are those that are acceptable in His sight, and who will stand with Him and He with *them* before the throne of grace. (no. 702–1)

Elsewhere it is stated that Jesus knew just how to speak to and teach children in ''those lessons given by Him as He spoke to the children in the childish *understanding* manner'' (no. 665–1). Apparently on such occasions Jesus' lessons were illustrated by stories ''of the lamb and . . . of the household pets'' (no. 665–1).

A number of references are made in the readings to the

ongoing effects, reaching even into incarnations in the twentieth century, of Jesus' having blessed, as well as more generally influenced, persons in his Palestinian ministry. A woman was told,

> As he gathered thee into His arms, materially, so is there—as ye abide in the presence of His love—that as may bring the security. For as goodness, as love lives on, so may thy body-soul realize . . . that blessing as ye magnify—in thy dealings with thy fellow men— "Inasmuch as ye do it unto the least of these, my little ones, ye do it unto me." (1877–1; compare Matt. 25: 40, 45)

This biblical theme of the solidarity of all human beings in spiritual being and in potential influence upon each other as with their Maker is repeatedly affirmed in the Cayce readings, as is the fact that love and goodness live on, that their effects are not lost in the ongoing processes of God's universe. We shall see in more detail later how evil is disposed of.

Another reading, given to a woman who was said also to have been among the children whom Jesus held "materially in His arms," speaks of Jesus' smile, "Thou wert there, my child! Thou felt His hand upon thy brow. Yea, ye saw the smile upon the Master's face. Yea, ye felt within thine very soul that strength that so oft keeps thee—in thine trials—in this very day" (no. 702–1).

JESUS AT BETHSAIDA

The Cayce readings include a considerable number of passages that may be grouped together as touching upon the experiences and teachings of Jesus that occurred at the town of Bethsaida by the Sea of Galilee. Bethsaida is said to have been "among the places often visited by the Master . . . this place where the Master liked to rest'' (1223–9).

A number of references are made to persons, including some in positions of authority, who entertained Jesus or "made the home His resting place" (no. 1223–4). One woman is described as giving of herself unstintingly to open her home "for the pleasure, the comfort, of a tired man—the Son of God" (no. 1223–4). This same reading speaks of "His face—worn at times"—words indicative of the toll taken by Jesus' strenuous physical activity and the constant giving out to others of the very depths of his mental and spiritual self in this itinerant ministry. In this very context, however, mention is made also of "that smile, that expression that brings the hope so necessary in the heart of the human—that there *is* the better way, there *is* safety in His presence, in the consciousness of the abiding faith in Him" (no. 1223–4). To this woman Jesus was a Friend as well as a Savior. She is said to have become "so closely associated with Jesus as to call Him by His name Jesus, not Master, until after His crucifixion" (1223–9).

The Cayce readings frequently describe with deeply compassionate feeling and understanding the existential needs of people and the common problems they meet within their lives. Thus those who heard Jesus at Bethsaida are cited as people "who looked for, who had come to expect that sometime, somewhere, God would hear the cry and answer those who were troubled by ills of body, turmoils of the struggles for life, for the meeting of the passions of the body of men, for the cries of the young for succor, for aid, yes, for bread" (no. 3660–1). It was to these that "He spoke gentle words—the sower went forth to sow. What are ye casting into the soil of life for those ye meet? Upon what character of soil seek ye to prepare, even in thine own life and heart and body" (no. 3660–1; compare Mark 4:1–20).

The relatively free handling of biblical passages, as seen here in interpreting Jesus' "parable of the soils," rephrasing the language—sometimes in a variety of expressions—in order to give the essence of the meaning and various modes of application, is common in the Cayce readings. We have seen also that they do not hesitate to cite extracanonical sayings of Jesus. Another expression of one such already cited is, "As He gave, those being on guard do not allow their houses, their own selves, or their mental abilities to be broken up" (no. 1968–1; compare Matt. 7:24–27; 12:25–29). On some occasions separate passages of the Bible are brought together to create a new focus of meaning: "As He has given so oft, it is here a little, there a little, line upon line, precept upon precept; *sowing* the fruits of the Spirit, *leaving* the fruition of same to God" (no. 1877–2; compare Isa. 28: 10, 13; Gal. 5:22–23; 6:8–9; Matt. 13:24–30).

In other cases quotations from the Scriptures are given, as so often in the fathers of the early church, either verbatim from the standard text available or as close paraphrases thereof. Thus we read, "as the Master gave Himself, 'Search the Scriptures, for in them ye think ye find eternal life and they are they that speak of me' " (5373–1; compare John 5: 39). Even here, however, the description of fact as given in the biblical account is subtly changed to a constructive admonition. The Cayce readings do not seem to aspire to verbal literalism even in reporting the teachings of Jesus. The essence of the meaning, or the intent, is evidently seen as the heart of the matter.

Further teachings identified in the readings as given by Jesus at Bethsaida include "those that the Master gave as to friendships, associations, forgiveness, the lack of common gossip about others . . . those warnings which were a part of the experience with Jesus of Nazareth" (no. 1223–9). He, "the lowly Nazarene" (1177–1), taught humility in a special way "to those who would become teachers and ministers in the experience of others" (1958–1). The readings are also frank in their identification of the personal and social limitations of Jesus' disciples at the time, a situation, this writer is poignantly reminded, not so different from this present time of writing. In one case we are told how a contemporary was inclined to dismiss these disciples as of no account, "because of the character or manner of livelihood of many of those who were proclaimed as disciples or adherents to those teachings'' (no. 1877–2).

Indeed, there were ''in the material many things that brought dissensions and strife among even the very elect, for the satisfying of material desires,'' even those of whom it is said, ''how glorious to have been among those . . . who were present when the Master of men, thy Brother, thy Savior yes, thine Intercessor before the throne of grace, as man—walked in the earth'' (no. 702–1).

The Cayce readings contain a number of references to ''the elect,'' a term that seems to denote primarily those called to particular roles in the service of the kingdom of God. It appears to carry no sense at all of an exclusive concept of eternal or ultimate salvation, as if some persons—in the Augustinian world view—were elected by divine decree before all creation to eternal salvation and others to eternal damnation (see Augustine, *Enchiridion* 107). We do, however, find references to those who were ''the closer followers of the Master'' (no. 3667–2; see also no. 1223–4). In the Cayce readings emphasis is repeatedly laid upon the fact that the Lord God ''calls all—whosoever will may come'' (no. 262–27, A-1), and Israel, who is ''the chosen of the Lord,'' ''means those who seek'' (no. 262–28, A-11). ''Be not unmindful that those met in the way are seekers also, and are the Israel of the Lord'' (262–30, A-6). ''He wills that all should come to the knowledge of His presence abiding with all'' (no. 262–33, A-2; compare 1 Tim. 2:4; 4:10; 2 Pet. 3: 9). This is ''the love of Him that calls that everyone should hear, should know, should understand'' (262–44).

We read also how ''it became necessary [for Jesus] to rebuke the disciples for their attempting to rebuke the peoples'' (5373–1). Yet Jesus' sternness at times was not dissociated from ''His laughter, His care, His thoughtfulness of others'' (no. 3342–1). We shall note later the ability of Jesus to laugh even amidst the sufferings of the last week of his earthly life. Indeed this aspect of Jesus' personal character—

his humor, his smile, his laughter—is a noteworthy contribution of the Cayce readings to our understanding of the person of Jesus the Christ. Furthermore, the spiritual truths that he taught, together with the influence of his person, "brought into the lives of those who followed in His way that of *joy*—though in service; *joy*—though in trial; *joy*—though in persecution for a cause and for a purpose" (no. 2043–1).

In another reading it is affirmed that, "His promises are sure, 'If ye seek me, I stand at the door and knock' " (no. 3089–1).

An admonition promptly follows, "Not that this is to become long-facedness, but the happiness—as the sorrows" is to have its place in the life of those who follow "the Way, the Truth and the Light . . . [for] He, in mercy, in grace, had overcome the world" (no. 4065–1; compare John 16:33). This same reading states that Jesus' affirmation of having overcome the world was already a part of Jesus' teaching at this time in his public ministry. A frequent admonition in the Cayce readings is to "keep the heart singing," as "there should be joyousness, gladness in the heart, in the speech . . . of each individual" (no. 262–46, A-3; 246–42).

9

THE CHILDREN'S BREAD

A NEW TESTAMENT passage that has long troubled commentators is the account of Jesus' healing the daughter of a woman in the district of Tyre and Sidon (the area is in modern Lebanon). The mother is called a Greek, a "Syrophoenician by birth," by Mark (7:24–30); a Canaanite by Matthew (15:21–28). The incident occurs on one of the several times when Jesus took his disciples with him on trips outside Jewish Palestine. In the Marcan version we read that in response to the mother's entreaty of Jesus that he heal her little daughter, who was "possessed by an unclean spirit," Jesus says, "Let the children first be fed, for it is not right to take the children's bread and throw it to the dogs." In Matthew the language is even harsher, "It is not fair to take the children's bread and throw it to the dogs."

This language seems to ascribe to Jesus ethnic prejudice of an extreme kind, a contemptuous evaluation of non-Jews with anthropological and theological bases. A singularly inept attempt to "explain" the contradiction—for Jesus, as we have seen, was warmly accepting of the persons of Gentiles in other accounts in the New Testament—is found in Jerome, who in the late fourth and early fifth centuries translated the Old and New Testaments into Latin, which became the Vulgate or official version of the Roman Catholic church. Jerome as a Roman and a Gentile commented, "O mira rerum conversio! Israel quondam filius, nos canes" (O wondrous reversal of things! Israel formerly the son, we the dogs). This affirmation of a later reversal of the objects of contempt is of course no solution to the problem of understanding Jesus' mind on this occasion.

In the Edgar Cayce readings there are at least six different references to this incident. In no case is the word "dogs" used by Jesus to denote the Syrophoenician woman or her compatriots. According to one reading the question Jesus asks his disciples—all Jews—was, "Must I give to those not of this household?" (no. 585–2). The word "household" evidently refers to the household of Israel; later this term came to be used of the Christian church as the household of faith (Gal. 6:10), or more broadly as the household of God (Eph. 2:19). According to the witness of the Gospel of Matthew, in the early part of his public ministry, Jesus understood his mission as focused on "the lost sheep of the house of Israel," even though we find in Matthew an early reference to Jesus' healing non-Jewish Gadarenes outside the borders of Jewish Palestine (Matt. 8:28–34). Some scholars believe that this expressed focus of concern represented Jesus' attempt to summon the people of Israel as a whole to their ancient calling to be a blessing to the whole of humanity, as revealed in the call of Abraham (Gen. 12:1–3). Such focus of course is no justification for the use of the term "dogs" to designate those whom one intends to help under God.

In the same Cayce reading, however, initiative and charm emerge not only from the Syrophoenician mother, as in the Marcan and Matthean accounts, where she answers, "Yes, Lord; yet even the dogs under the table eat the children's crumbs" (Mark 7:28, or as in Matt. 15:27, "Yes, Lord, yet even the dogs eat the crumbs that fall from their master's table"). Admittedly, in the New Testament versions the dialogue forms a consistent whole; but in the Cayce readings a different tone emerges on Jesus' part, for it is said, "the

Master put his hands upon the entity and loves the entity"
(no. 585–2).

In all the readings that refer to this incident, the word
"dogs" is used only by the mother, as in one case, "Yes,
Lord, but even the dogs eat of the crumbs from the master's
table" (no. 1159–1); or in an other, "Doth not the servants—
even the dogs—eat at the master's table?" (no. 2364–1). In
both of these readings the response of Jesus as given is similar: "I have have not found so great a faith, no, not in
Israel" (no. 1159–1; 2364–1; compare Matt. 8:10, Luke 7:
9). In Matthew 15:28 Jesus is described as answering the
mother most warmly, "O woman, great is your faith! Be it
done for you as you desire."

Mark 7:29 gives us language of Jesus somewhat less en-
thusiastic. "For this saying you may go your way; the demon
has left your daughter." The consensus of contemporary biblical scholarship would appear to attribute the harsh language
of these passages to the fact that there was a strong tendency
in the early Palestinian church to restrict its mission to Jews
and Jewish proselytes (compare Acts 10:1–48, where the
conversion of Peter from this mentality is graphically described).

The readings all agree with the biblical accounts that the
daughter was healed instantly by Jesus. These readings twice
refer to Jesus as "the Holy One" (no. 2364–1; no. 105–2).
And strong emphasis is laid upon the abiding effects of his
ministry in this place among the people who are said in a
reading to be "of a mixed race" (no. 1159–1). Jesus is also
said to have blessed the entire household of the woman, and
brief reference is made to the fact that the historic accounts
of this event have "been diverted by many of the writers of
same" (no. 105–2). In the same reading, immediately following this observation, we find a direct quotation of Jesus:
"He that believeth in me, or that cometh to me, I will in no
wise cast out, for even as I am in the Father and ye in me,
we are then one with the Father that doeth His will" (compare John 6:35, 37; 17:21).

The intent of the whole reading is clearly such as to refuse to ascribe to Jesus any kind of racial, cultural, or religious partiality. The Cayce readings frequently refer to the Jews as that "peculiar people" in the old sense of the English word meaning "distinctive" and thereby indicate something of the distinctive aspects of the divine calling and mission of "the people of the Hebrews." But the readings are one with the best of contemporary biblical scholarship in affirming the earlier universal covenants of God with the whole of humanity, indeed "between God and every living creature of all flesh that is upon the earth" (compare Gen. 3:15; 9:8–19; 12:1–3). To my knowledge the readings never speak of the Jews as the sole objects of God's love and care, or as the exclusive beneficiaries of his salvation, however this last term be defined.

Significantly a somewhat similar understanding of this biblical account can be found in *The Aquarian Gospel of Jesus the Christ*, a book written in the United States around the turn of this century. The significance emerges not merely from the content itself but (in connection with consideration of Edgar Cayce) also from the fact that the author, Levi H. Dowling, claimed to have received the contents of his book through clairvoyant means. In any case, in Dowling's account Jesus responds to the woman's appeal—he had come to the district primarily to pray, not to teach—by first recalling a common proverb, "It is not meet that one should give the children's bread to dogs." The woman's response is cited as in the biblical accounts, and then, before healing the "obsessed" daughter, Jesus says, "Such faith I have not seen, no, not among the Jews; she is not serf, not dog."

We have already taken note of the Cayce readings' mention of Jesus' blessing children and then using them as "sermon objects" in teaching adults, "Except ye become as little children, ye shall in no wise enter in" (no. 1532–1; compare Mark 10:15, and parallels). It seems appropriate at this point to reintroduce the subject, partly because of the numerous references to the incident in the readings and partly because several of the teachings that Jesus is said to have given in this context are particularly appropriate as introductory to the Cayce accounts of Jesus' treatment of Mary Magdalene.

The readings in this context particularly stress as a model for adults the quickness of children to forgive and forget. Thus Jesus is described as "one that drew children to Him and made of them and their lives an illustration of the manner in which people—men, women, everywhere—must accept those activities of their fellow associates. For if one would be forgiven as a child, one must forgive those that would— or do—err against self" (no. 857–1). The meaning of the phrase, cited as a condition of our own acceptance, "Unless ye become as a little child," is explained in another reading: "Unless you become as open-minded, unless you can get mad and fight and then forgive and forget—for it is the nature of man to fight, while it is the nature of God to forgive . . . 'As ye forgive, so are ye forgiven.' As ye treat thy fellow man ye are treating thy Maker" (no. 3395–3; compare Luke 3:37). (The readings, of course, do not mean this kind of phrase—"it is the nature of God to forgive"—to be understood in the light, even flippant, sense of Heinrich Heine's *"Dieu me pardonnera. C'est son métier"* (God will forgive me. It's his business).)

The point of reciprocal responsibility is then repeated in the reading to emphasize the fact that forgiveness, by God or one's fellow beings, is not to be assumed as operating automatically regardless of our response but is only operative and functional when accompanied by our willingness to forgive others, by our own openness to correction and change of character and lifestyle.

The Cayce readings emphasize that Jesus taught not "dogmatic influences of an orthodox activity" (no. 1401–1) but "principles" that are in fact descriptive of cosmic process even as they are expressions of divine will. The readings therefore do not hesitate to give full weight to the so-called "hard" sayings of Jesus. For example, along with many, many quotations or rephrasings of "Whatever a man sows, that he will also reap" (Gal. 6:7), there are frequent references to Jesus' teaching "with what measure ye mete, it is measured to thee again. Even as He, the Master, gave, the faults we find in others are reflected in thine own mirror of life. And as He gave, 'Cast the beam out of thine eye that ye may see to take the mote from thy brother's eye' " (no. 3395–2; compare Matt. 7:1–5).

The principle of sowing and reaping, of compensation as Ralph Waldo Emerson preferred to call it, or of karma as is frequently heard these days, is indeed seen in the Cayce readings as a divine, cosmic principle. Its operation, however, is never perceived as an iron law that is unbreakable or from which there is no escape. As we shall discuss more fully later, the law of grace takes precedence over the law of karma. Thus in a reading that refers to Jesus' parable of the seed sown in various conditions of soil (compare Mark 4:1–25), the individual addressed is squarely told that in a previous incarnation he had been among those whose "ideals and persecutions were choked out" as a result of persecutions and hardships suffered in regard to material things (no. 3308–1). The effects of this response still abide in some measure, but they are to be taken as basis for a lesson to be learned. And as part of the way out the admonition was given, "less and less of self, and more and more of the Spirit of truth [compare John 14:17] should be in thy ministering, in thy attempting to direct others."

With reference to the meaning of human suffering, the entity was instructed to remember the experience of Jesus himself, "Though He were the Son, yet learned He obedience through the things which He suffered" (compare Heb. 5:8). In addition to the development of character to be gained through such experiences, the profound point is made that relationship with our Maker hovers over our participation in the entire process, "Count thyself then rather as being remembered, when ye suffer for His sake" (no. 3308–1).

In addition to so-called "hard" sayings, the New Testament records Jesus as knowing anger (for example, Mark 3:

5), which we may perhaps appropriately describe as anger permeated with the pain of compassion. The Cayce readings emphasize, however, the overall positive and constructive nature as well as effect of Jesus' teaching. Thus we read of one "not only being thrilled by the presence but by the words of the Master as He gave what ye call the Beatitudes" (Matt. 5:1–12). This same person is told that the proper response to hearing those words of Jesus is "the kind word, the patient word, the pressing of the hand upon the brow of those who are with fever, yea those who are troubled in heart there may be brought comfort by the [same] words" (no. 5089–2).

THE WOMAN CAUGHT IN THE ACT OF ADULTERY

There is a famous passage in the Gospel of John (7:53–8:11) about a woman caught in the act of adultery. When brought as a test case to Jesus, she was treated with remarkable compassion by him in the face of critics hostile both to him and to her. Although this story is found in a few old Latin texts of the New Testament, it does not appear in any Greek manuscript earlier than the sixth century. Also its location in manuscripts varies; it is sometimes placed at the end of the Gospel of John, instead of in the seventh and eighth chapters, or after Luke 21:38. There is, however, a wide scholarly consensus that this passage is an authentic account. The woman, incidentally, is not identified.

The Cayce readings, however, say that this passage is actually based on two different incidents in the ministry of Jesus and that in one case the woman involved is Mary Magdalene. She is also said to be the Mary who was the sister of Lazarus and Martha (compare John 11:2; 12:3; Luke 7:36–50). This identification may indeed be inferred from the New Testament gospels but is not explicitly made there. The other woman, according to Cayce, had been primarily associated with Roman soldiers. We shall consider these incidents separately, giving, as the readings do, weight to the accounts that relate to Mary, whose role became significant in the growing Christian movement.

According to the Cayce readings, Mary Magdalene was a courtesan who offered her services to Roman officers and civilians as well as to Jews (no. 295–8); and prostitutes of this class sometimes used their skills "for the gaining of information of various sorts and natures" (no. 5749–9). Since the Cayce text says specifically that such was *not* the case with the other woman (who was also compassionately aided by Jesus), and refrains from making such a statement in the case of Mary, it may be proper to infer that Mary was engaged in some kind of espionage activity, in behalf of the Jews, as a part of her profession at that time. In any case the readings say that because of her activities Mary was separated from her family in Bethany, and only after her experience with Jesus was she reunited with them (no. 295–8).

Mary's family background appears to have been one of considerable distinction at that time and place. She, together with her brother and sister, are said to have been closely associated with the disciples—later apostles—James and John (no. 5749–9). In this context we should note that the Cayce readings state that John "was the wealthiest of the disciples of the Christ. His estate would be counted in the present [A.D. 1933], in American money, as being near to a quarter of a million dollars . . . he was a power" among both the Romans and the Jews (no. 295–8; John's brother James was killed by King Herod in A.D. 42. Compare Acts 12:1–2).

The readings state that the incident with Mary occurred first, in the early portion of Jesus' public ministry. The second case, of the younger maid "taken in the act with the Roman soldiery," occurred "*after* there had been the reuniting of Martha, Lazarus, and Mary" (no. 5749–9). Mary is said to have been brought before the Jewish council, or Sanhedrin, and "the whole council or court at the time asked that, according to the law, the woman be stoned" (no. 295–

8). According to the Old Testament (Lev. 20:10 and Deut. 22:22) both of the guilty parties in a case of adultery should be sentenced to death. It is noteworthy that in the New Testament account (John 7:53–8:11) the woman's accusers do not bring the responsible other party or parties to account at all. If Mary had in fact served the interests of the Jewish establishment as a spy, we may perhaps infer that something had happened to force their hand, to compel them to take action against Mary, against their will.

Mary is said to have been "twenty-three years old when the Christ cleansed her from the seven devils: avarice, hate, self-indulgence, and those of the kindred selfishnesses, [from] hopelessness and blasphemy" (no. 295–8). This language constitutes a specific identification of the Mary of this incident with "Mary, called Magdalene," as cited in the Gospel of Luke (8:2). Mary is described as "a body five feet four inches in height, weight a hundred and twenty-one pounds—in the general. Hair almost red. The eyes were blue. The features were those impelled both from the Grecian and Jewish ancestry" (no. 295–8).

The reading goes on to say that Jesus at that time wrote in the sand "that which condemned each individual, as each looked over His arm—or as He wrote" (no. 295–8; compare John 8:6). Older readers may recall that, while the Johannine account does not specify what Jesus wrote in the sand, *The King of Kings*, the famous epic movie of the life of Jesus directed by Cecil B. de Mille two generations ago, portrays this incident with precisely the same insight into the content of Jesus' writing as does the Cayce reading. The reading then states that what Jesus said to Mary was, "Neither do I condemn thee—Neither do *I* condemn thee." This event became for Mary an experience of "cleansing of the body-mind"— "an awakening." The experience is also connected in the reading with the problem of self-condemnation, and the woman who asked Cayce for the reading and was said herself to have been Mary Magdalene is specifically told for her present needs, "Do not condemn self!" (no. 295–8).

The Cayce readings frequently refer to self-condemnation as a mental and moral problem as serious as the condemnation of others. In this case the person addressed is told, "Condemning self is condemning the abilities of the Master . . . the Christ, [who] manifested life in the earth" (no. 295–8). In this reading the mode of Jesus' manifestation of life—which is given in the context of affirmation that "God is God of the *living*, NOT of the dead! . . . Life, then, is God"—was "through not only the material manifestations that were given in the ministry but in laying aside the life. As He gave, 'I *give* my life, I give it of myself, and I take it of myself' " (no. 295–8; compare John 10:17–18).

As we have seen, the Cayce readings do not offer a totally monistic worldview, as if all were one without distinction. They frequently affirm the fact of the distinctiveness of the consciousness of each human being, even if such distinctiveness is not absolute. The life, however, that makes such consciousness possible—this latter is also seen as identical with our soul, which is that made in the image of God (compare Gen. 1:26–27)—is created by God, indeed is an emanation of God, so as to make it possible to say that God is life (compare John 14:6).

The thirty-year-old American woman who requested this series of readings was told in her first reading, regarding self-condemnation, "Blot *this* from *thine* experience, *through* Him who maketh all things possible" (no. 295–1). She later asked regarding her own role, "Did the entity repay any fraction of the debt owed the Master while He was in the earth?" The answer came back in forthright terms:

That's impossible! . . .
So in any attempt to repay—there can be no repay! But when one lives the life that *manifests* the Christ life, love, joy, peace, harmony, grace, glory, the *joy* is in the life of the Master as He manifests—and manifested—life in the earth. (no. 295–8)

After this experience "of the saving grace in the love of the Christ, the Savior of men" (no. 295–8), Mary returned, the readings say, to her family in Bethany near Jerusalem, where "those two vital forces of such different natures— Mary and Martha—and Lazarus" (no. 2787–1) made of their home "the center from which most of the activities of the disciples took place . . ." from that time and in that area (no. 295–8). With reference to "the cleansing power" manifested in both the raising of Lazarus (which we shall discuss later) and the restoration of Mary, we are told that "All those, then, that were cleansed by Him have been called—are called— for special missions, for activities in each experience in and among men that they . . . may demonstrate, may give, the blessings to many" (no. 295–8).

This, then, is the Mary of whom "the Master said, 'She hath chosen the better part' " (no. 295–1; compare Luke 10: 42). The Cayce readings follow the tradition of the Gospel of John in identifying Mary with the woman who anointed the feet of Jesus with costly ointment but remains nameless in the synoptic gospels (compare John 12:1–8, Matt. 26:6– 13, Mark 14:3–9; Luke 7:36–50). With reference to Jesus' words "Wherever my Gospel is preached, her works will be spoken of" (compare Mark 14:9 and parallels), this reading comments, "What a heritage!" (no. 295–1).

The readings state further that the home of Mary and Martha became a center of support for the activities of the disciples particularly of Judean background, as contrasted with the perhaps larger group of Galilean disciples. Also, after the return from Galilee following the ascension of Jesus, when Mary, the mother of Jesus, became "a dweller in the house or home of John . . ." this John, the beloved disciple, is said to have "joined with those in Bethany. . . ." "Hence the associations of Mary and John became the closest after this (we are speaking of Mary, the sister of Martha)." Whether this statement means that Mary, the sister of Martha, married John is not clear, but it is at least possible, as the same reading later speaks of Mary Magdalene as being part of John's household along with Mary, the mother of Jesus, and the sister of the mother of James and John (no. 295–8).

In this context reference is made to a journey to "what would be called their *summer* home . . ." on the shores of the Lake of Gennesaret (the sea of Galilee), which also became a center of support for Christian workers of every kind who "came and went" at that period (no. 295–8). In the same reading Mary, the sister of Martha, is said to have lived "some twenty and two years" after her cleansing.

The other incident occurred later in Jesus' public ministry, and is similar to Mary's experience in essence. A young woman was "brought before the Master in the temple . . . condemned as one taken in adultery; and because of the judgment passed upon that entity according to the law, the peoples or the high priests or those of the Sanhedrin declared that He must make a statement" (no. 1436–2). This particular reading agrees with the interpretation of the German New Testament scholar Joachim Jeremias that the woman had already been judged and convicted by the Sanhedrin and Jesus was being asked to give his view of the proper punishment. In any case, Jesus was here faced with a distinct dilemma. There is some evidence that about the year A.D. 30 the Romans took away from the Sanhedrin the legal right of executing, as distinguished from recommending, capital punishment. This is the view of the author(s) of the Fourth Gospel at the time of writing (John 18:31). If such be the case, the Jewish leadership may have been conniving in a plan to bypass the Roman proscription with a mob lynching, as occurred later with the stoning of the first Christian martyr, Stephen (Acts 6:1–7:60). The dilemma for Jesus, however, lay in the fact that if he were to forgive the woman and request her release, he would violate the clear ordinance of the Mosaic law (Lev. 20:10; Deut. 22:22), even though the same law required that both the guilty parties be stoned. If he were to order the woman to be stoned, he would be asking for trouble with the Romans (as in the similar dilemma of the Roman coin described in Mark 12:13–17).

This reading says that "He gave, 'Let him that is without sin cast the first stone.' Let him that has been guiltless make the first move for the fulfilling of the *letter* of the law" (1436–2; compare John 8:7). Perceptive readers will note that the first sentence of this last quotation is an almost verbatim quotation of John 8:7, while the second gives essentially the same meaning in altered language in the mode of traditional Hebraic poetic parallelism. The second sentence also may conceivably be an authentic word of Jesus.

The Cayce readings say that in both cases of the women taken in adultery Jesus stooped and wrote on the ground. In the latter instance in the temple Jesus wrote words that called for "the expression of mercy and not sacrifice" (no. 5749–9; compare Matt. 9:13; Hos. 6:6), words that also brought "the awakening in the heart of the entity of hope" (no. 1436–2). In the earlier instance, "That written was that which made the accusers recognize their *own* activities" (no. 5749–9). Here in the temple, with this awakening of hope, "as the cry came, 'Master, what sayest thou?' the answer came, 'I condemn thee not, daughter—go and sin no more' " (no. 1436–2; compare John 8:11).

This reading goes on to say, "Is it any wonder, then, that those days that followed made for a remolding of the entity? Though the entity kept afar, and not until after those periods when the persecutions began did she venture to come nigh unto those that were classed or called of the household of faith" (no. 1436–2). This girl apparently felt that even those of the household of faith created by Jesus himself were not open enough to take her into their fellowship until they, too, had been brought low in the eyes of the world. A reading referring to Mary Magdalene expresses very clearly the attitude that prevailed at first in at least some of the disciples. "With the return of Mary after the conversion and the casting out of the demons—this brought even greater confusion to the entity. For to the entity, how *could* anyone who had been *such* a person—or who had so disregarded persons except for the material gains—become an honored one among those, or in association with a household of ones, such as Lazarus and Martha'' (no. 993–5).

Reading no. 1436–2 continues, "But to have had the words direct from the Master of masters, the Teacher of teachers, 'I do not condemn thee,' *has* meant, must mean, in the experience of the entity, that which words cannot portray." The only appropriate response to such gracious mercy, the reading says, is to express the same in relationship to others, through "the deeds of the body, the desire of the mind, to bring hope, faith, *in* that Lord, that Master, who is able to *save* unto the utmost, and who hath given to all, 'My peace I leave *with* you, my peace I give *unto* you.' '' It is also stated that after refusing to condemn the woman, Jesus said to her, "Be thou merciful, even as I have shown and give thee mercy." Following this admonition there is given advice that is as valid today as it was during the Master's time:

In the life of intolerability in the experience, cannot the entity find in the heart of self to say, even as He, 'They know not what they do,' and to give the cup of water, to give the healing in the hands, to give the cherishment to those that are sad?

To those that are joyous give them more joy, in that praise be given to Him who maketh life to all that seek to know His face. (no. 1436–2; compare Luke 23:34; Matt. 10:42)

The readings state that Jesus was questioned at different times by different groups in the contemporary spectrum of Jewish schools of faith and practice, now by the Pharisees, now by the Sadducees, or "by those in Roman authority" (no. 5749–9). One reading paints the scene in the temple with vivid contrasts, showing Jesus facing the questioning Sadducees, as "the experience when before those in penal law or authority, those with their pomp and glory—yet He in *all*

His glory, His face shining as only from the Father-God itself!'' (no. 1436–2).

This use of the neuter personal pronoun with reference to the Father-God should not be understood to mean that the Cayce readings affirm God to be ultimately impersonal. As we have seen already in this collection of materials, the readings teach that God is sublimely personal, that he is both self-conscious and conscious of us, and that he seeks companionship as the Maker with his creation, above all with the souls that he created in the beginning (compare no. 1567–2; no. 1458–1; no. 5064–1). ''He cares!'' (no. 1567–2). One occasionally finds use of the neuter gender with reference to God among mainstream theologians of the early Christian church, as with Gregory of Nyssa in his work *On the Soul and the Resurrection*, composed in A.D. 380, with intent to suggest ''transpersonal'' dimensions of the Godhead that transcend our limited human experiences of the personal. In the Cayce readings the male personal pronoun is used much more frequently than the neuter, especially is the word Father used, although, as we have seen, the term Creative Force, or Creative Forces (compare the Hebrew plural usage of Elohim for God, as in Gen. 1:1–2:4a; 12:1 ff.), is also frequently found. Significantly the readings, like some Gnostic Christians in the early church, also use the term ''the Mother-God,'' or ''Father-Mother God'' as other appropriate designations for the Most-High, who is always seen as ultimately one (no. 945–1; no. 281–39). (See Elaine Pagels's *The Gnostic Gospels*, especially *The Apocryphon of John*.) Another reading discusses the issue in the following way, ''How personal is thy God? Just as personal as ye will let Him be! How close is the Christ as was manifested in the physical body Jesus? Just as close, just as dear as ye will let Him be!'' (no. 1158–9).

''This was the Holy One, who honored woman that she might, too, be equal with man in the redemption of man [generic] from the wiles of the devil, or the wiles of him who would cause man or woman to err in any manner'' (no. 5231–1).

10

THE TRANSFIGURATION
EXPERIENCE

RELATIVELY FEW DETAILS are given in the Cayce readings regarding the experience of Jesus and three disciples who conversed in visionary mode on the mount of transfiguration with the two greatest figures of the Hebrew religious tradition, the lawgiver Moses and the prophet Elijah. One statement is that "He had withdrawn in the mount that there might be material evidence in the flesh to His faithful three [Peter, James, and John]" (no. 3216–1; compare Mark 9:2–13 and parallels). It is also stated that after this experience it was difficult for the disciples to understand why they themselves could not heal just as Jesus did. Another reading asks, "Did Moses and Elias give strength to Him, or gain strength from Him?" The context of this question emphasizes that Jesus taught and manifested the fact that the kingdom of God is within and "it is not a dependence upon the powers without!"

This reading also has a further statement about human interiority as of prior importance but yet requiring external expression. "It is *within* that there is the kingdom of heaven! The kingdom of *God* is without but is manifested in how it is reacting upon *thee*—by the manner in which ye mete to thy associates day by day that concept of that light which rises within!" (no. 877–27). The reading as a whole makes it clear that the source of Jesus' power was the Father abiding within and not worldly powers or supernal spirits, however worthy they severally may be (no. 877–27).

A point of considerable significance is that another reading rephrases Mark 9:1–2 as follows: " 'There be some standing here that will see me come in my glory.' And He taketh with Him, Peter, James, and John and goeth into the mount, and *there* was transfigured before them" (no. 478–4; compare no. 877–27). Since Mark 9:1 contains the statement, "There are some standing here who will not taste death before they see the kingdom of God come with power," this Cayce reading may indicate that Jesus understood the transfiguration experience as one mode of his glorification.

This same reading has an instructive discussion of the role of "the nine left in the valley" at the time Jesus took only three of the twelve chief disciples (later termed apostles) to share with him the experience on the mount of transfiguration. The question is asked, "Were they not great preachers, great ministers? Did they not have a close contact with the very Truth and Life itself? Yet it is not that He had departed, not that He was withdrawn." We have here an affirmation of the meaning and value of the life and work of those of the twelve who were not taken along to participate in this momentous experience. They are not to be less thought of, either as persons or in terms of their effectiveness in the ministry of the Gospel, because they were not among the three. A brief statement is made that they, for whatever reason, did not have at that particular time the effective power to heal that they had had formerly or would have later. The point of the discussion, however, seems to be that Peter, James, and John were chosen to share the experience for "strategical" or "formally functional" reasons that are not to be understood as implying personal worth in the three superior to that of the others "left in the valley."

A further question is asked in the same reading with reference to the results in their personal lives of Peter, James, and John having had the privilege of sharing in the experience: "Did it take from the activities or add to the activities of Peter, James, and John—their being in the Presence? Peter denied. John held to himself. James—by his very exertion—Herod laid his hands upon him" (compare Mark 14:66–72; John 21:20–24; Acts 12:1–2). This reading tells the man of forty-five to whom it was addressed that these matters should be lessons in his own life experience, that it should not disturb him whether he "may be either upon the mount in thine experience with Him, or in the valley with the nine," for he was still "of Him" (no. 478–4). The highest meaning of life, we are apparently being told, is not in sublime religious experiences nor in exalted callings, but in faithfulness to the task at hand whatever and wherever that may be. The Lord of life is present with his grace and glory in comparable authenticity in both valley and mount.

Another reading, in speaking of the statement of Peter on the mount of transfiguration—"Let us make here a tabernacle"—goes on to ask, "What indeed is thy tabernacle? It is thy body, thy mind, thy soul! Present them, therefore, as things holy, acceptable unto Him who *is* the Giver of all good and perfect gifts!" This in turn is in order that he "who thought it not robbery to be equal with God yet made Himself of *no* estate . . . might enter into the holy of holies with thee in thy *own* tabernacle!" (no. 877–27; compare 1 Cor. 3:16; Rom. 12:1; Jas. 1:17; Phil. 2:6). In another reading we find a brief indication of one meaning of the transfiguration experience, "What saw they? A glorified body? The glory of the body brought what? Communion of saints!" (no. 262–87). These words remind us that "the communion of saints" does include a mode of relationship with those who have passed on and that Jesus did talk with "the dead" on the mount of transfiguration (compare 2 Pet. 2:15).

THE RAISING OF LAZARUS

There are numerous accounts and references in the Cayce readings to Jesus' raising Lazarus from the dead. This event is described in the New Testament only in the Gospel of John, but there in considerable detail (John 11:1–57). Jesus' relationship to this family in Bethany, a town only a short distance from Jerusalem, was clearly special (compare Luke 10:38–42).

The readings state that Jesus went there often, to "the rest place in Bethany" (no. 966–1; see also no. 993–5). This special relationship is affirmed even in the context of statements revealing the universality "of that love shown in that experience to those peoples, wherever the *Master* walked" (no. 2466–1). Lazarus is called "the brother to those whom the Lord loved" (no. 1924–1), a statement reminding us of the biblical sentence, "Now Jesus loved Martha and her sister and Lazarus" (John 11:5). The readings contain several references to the fact that Jesus "wept with Mary, Martha, and that household" (no. 993–5); "He—the friend—wept with those of His friends in the face of criticism, in the company of the great and the near great . . ." (no. 2787–1; compare John 11:33–36).

The family of Lazarus was evidently one of distinction in the society of the time, although perhaps not wealthy, as we read of "the little house in Bethany" (no. 2466–1; see also no. 1924–1). No reference is made to his father in the readings, to my knowledge, nor in the Bible. His mother, however, is said to have been "a close adherent of the Essene thought yet of the orthodox group" (no. 993–5). This statement appears to mean that his mother's formal associations were with the religious establishment of the time but that her personal faith and worldview were closer to the Essenic expression of the traditional faith of Israel. The whole family, however, had come to be, like Lazarus, "the friend, the companion, of those who loved His [Jesus'] name, who loved His manner" (no. 1924–1). Lazarus is said to have been "ill of a fever—what today would be called the slow fever, or typhoid—and there was the eventual death" (no. 993–5).

The Cayce readings agree with the biblical account that Lazarus was "four days in the tomb" (no. 3656–1; see also no. 5148–2; compare John 11:17). The actual raising of Lazarus is described—and interpreted—with various phrases and statements, "To Lazarus we find He called, 'Come forth!' " (no. 1158–14; compare John 11:43). A contemporary application is offered by the sleeping Cayce: "He stands at the door and knocks [compare Rev. 3:20], even as He did at the tomb, as He called Lazarus to come forth. For He overcame death, hell *and* the grave by His wholly trusting in the love of the Father" (no. 993–5).

Lazarus is said to have lived after his being raised from the dead "only until the first of the rebellions arise" (no. 295–8), perhaps a reference to the uprising against the Romans led by a man named Theudas about ten years after Jesus' crucifixion (compare Acts 5:34–39; Josephus, *Antiquities of the Jews*, XX, 5, 1).

Reading no. 993–5, which explains the significance not only of the raising of Lazarus but also of Jesus' own resurrection, gives a representative Cayce statement of the proper relationship among body, mind, and soul, or spirit, in human life on earth. "The spirit is willing, the flesh is weak [compare Mark 14:38]—but hate not the flesh for its weakness; and know that in materiality they are one, that must coordinate as the body, the mind and the soul, if one would be creative in body, mind, or spirit . . . It is only as ye apply that ye know that ye grow" (no. 993–5).

This positive attitude of the Cayce readings toward materiality (not, to be sure, toward materialism!) is revealed in a richly suggestive reading given in the year 1937. A woman had asked the sleeping Cayce, "If I believe that God within is capable of meeting my every need, how can I justify my going to an osteopath for treatments?" The answer was,

How did Jesus, the Son, the Christ, justify Himself in telling the man that was healed from leprosy to "Go, show thyself to the priest and offer the sacrifice that was commanded by Moses" [compare Mark 1:40–45]?

Did the man remain healed because of the act or because God spoke and was sufficient?

Now, when Lazarus was dead, yea, when Jairus's daughter lay dead, He spoke and they were aroused. Yet He took *her* by the hand and commanded that food and drink be given [compare Mark 5:35–43].

For in the material world, material responses must apply to the material being.

To Lazarus we find He called, "Come forth!" yet he [Lazarus] was not able to unbind himself. (no. 1158–14)

This emphasis upon the appropriateness upon earth of the use of material means and measures, together with utter trust in God, is seen in another reading, which also stresses the need for human cooperation, both individual and corporate, with the Divine in order to achieve truly effective results. This reading describes the raising of Lazarus in the following way:

When He spoke, death itself gave up that it had claimed, even though the sister had warned that there had not been the embalming as had been the purposes of many. Instantly the activity brought life. For He *is* life. He *is* health, He *is* beauty, He *is*—not was, not will be—but is! For He having overcome death, hell, and the grave, He is justified before God in giving to him who believes, who is in accord, that, "If ye ask in my name, believing," doing, being that ye ask for, that shall be done unto thee [compare John 14:13–14; 16:23–24].

Yet with the breaking of the bonds of death, the breaking of the material bond, the binding about the head, must needs be done by others. (no. 5749–16)

This same reading then proceeds to offer further comment on the appropriateness of human cooperation, as well as of

material means, on this earthly plane, "There is ever, then—
in thy material associations, in thy seeking for help, love,
health, understanding for thy brother—*something*, some effort on their part as well as *thine*. But 'where two or three
are gathered together in my name, there will I be in the midst
of them' " (no. 5749–16; compare Matt. 18:20).

It is noteworthy that the sisters of Lazarus had refused to
agree to the embalming of their brother, a process that no
doubt would have involved the draining of his blood and,
humanly speaking, would have thus rendered much more difficult the restoration of his life. The biblical account only
hints at the condition of Lazarus's body, which at the time
of Jesus' arrival at the tomb was already giving forth a distinct odor (John 11:39). This refusal on the part of the sisters
suggests that they had faith and hope that Jesus would somehow be able to help their brother (compare John 11:3, 22).

Another reading offers us further information on the interrelationship of the physical, mental, and spiritual aspects
of life.

> Though there may be mechanical or medicinal appli-
> cations for the welfare of the physical body, these are
> to attune the body to that consciousness which makes
> or brings it aware of its relationship to the spiritual, or
> God-Force. Just as the clay, the spittle upon the eyes
> of the blind had that effect to bring the awareness of
> the presence of the Creative Force, or God, to those
> granulated lids in the experience of that individual. (no.
> 2812–1 [compare John 9:1–41])

In the set of readings that refer to Lazarus, we find several
comments about Judas Iscariot that shed light on Jesus' posture toward the larger political, social, and economic activities of his day. Judas was not alone in his views and activity,
but had a number of supporters in the particular program that
he apparently sought to have Jesus carry out. One reading
states that "Those groups about Judas sought to proclaim

Jesus as the deliverer of the peoples from that bondage [of the Romans], that taxation'' (no. 1179–7). The same reading gives us Jesus' response to such plans in citing his ''rebukings of the peoples that were especially about Judas at that time.'' This is of course to say that Jesus forthrightly rejected plans for political revolution by physical violence. The New Testament gospel accounts, we may recall, reveal Jesus' consistent emphasis upon the prior importance of the interiority of human beings. He clearly asked for social, economic, and political justice from all; but perhaps he sensed the Jews could be worse off under their own rulers—as they were at that time (Caiaphas, Annas, and so on)—than under the Romans (compare Luke 13:31–32; Mark 14–15, and parallels).

Further insight on this problem is given in the same reading, which emphasizes with regard to ''Him—who is the Way, the Truth, the Light'' that this is ''the truth that maketh men free indeed, though they may be under the shadow of service to a higher power materially.'' This profoundly significant affirmation of the power of the Risen Christ to liberate—to be truly and significantly effective, helpful in the lives of human beings no matter what their political, economic, or social circumstances may be, even, evidently, without structural changes in these circumstances—appears in the same reading as a statement of the primary purposes for which Jesus had entered into the world: ''The purposes for which His entrance into the world had been [made were], as He gave, not for self, not for material gain, but that *all* should know the truth that would make *all* men free under *every* circumstance in a material plane'' (no. 1179–7). ''His [was the] ability to roll back death, even to defy same and to give others a greater hope'' (no. 2519–8).

These statements give us in succinct form affirmations regarding the understandings of divine providence to be found in the Cayce readings. This is that there are specific opportunities—however insignificant or even invisible they may appear at any one time and place—that continue to be given in the lives of every human being or corporate group on this earthly plane, or in other realms. Thus we read elsewhere, "Do not count any condition lost. Rather make each the stepping-stone to higher things, remembering that God does not allow us to be tempted beyond that we are able to bear and comprehend, if we will but make our wills one with His" (no. 900–44; compare 1 Cor. 10:13).

This excerpt is an example of the relatively frequent instances in the Cayce readings where one verse or more is quoted from the Bible—sometimes verbatim, sometimes with variations from the common text, as the early church fathers often did—in such a way as to give at the same time an explication of its meaning or to suggest a mode of application of its truth. For example, this Pauline verse (1 Cor. 10:13) is often quoted, but with a variety of concluding phrases, or of combinations with other verses: "God hath not willed that any soul should perish, but hath with every temptation, every trial, every disappointment made a way of escape or for correcting same" (no. 1567–2; compare 1 Tim. 2:4; 4:10; 2 Pet. 3:9); "He hath not willed that any soul should perish, but has with each temptation, each trial, prepared a way of understanding or escape" (no. 2081–1). "He hath not willed that any soul should perish, but hath with each temptation prepared a manner in which each soul may meet itself" (no. 1663–2). "He hath not willed that any soul should perish, and thus again and again comes that opportunity" (no. 3581–1). "For the Father has not willed that any soul should perish, and is thus mindful that each soul has again and again—and yet again—the opportunity for making its path straight" (no. 2021–1). "For when the souls of men had wandered away, He—not willing that any soul should perish—has prepared a way through which, by which, they each may find their way again to that companionship, that relationship with the Creative Forces" (no. 1458–1; compare 2 Cor. 5:18–20). "He hath not willed that any soul should perish, but hath with each temptation prepared a way, a manner, through which each soul may become aware of its faults, its virtues—magnifying the virtues, minimizing the

faults [of self, as of others]—that one may come to the perfect knowledge of one's relationship to the Creative Influences, called God'' (no. 2397–1). ''Know first, the Lord thy
God hath not tempted any soul, He hath not given any soul
that it may not meet. And He hath prepared a way of escape
for each soul if it will but harken to that voice deep within''
(no. 417–8; compare Jas. 1:13–15; 1 Kings 19:12).

A fine statement of these principles is given in the well-
known volumes that attempt to summarize the Cayce readings as a guide to spiritual growth and effective daily living,
A Search for God: ''May we never think that the opportunity
has passed, for God's mercy is without limit . . . *Today* is the
acceptable day of the Lord! It is never too late for us to
begin.'' Or as reading no. 333–6 puts it, ''There are *always*
opportunities! Opportunities are *never* withdrawn.'' And the
way to make use of the opportunities is given again and again
in the Cayce readings. ''If ye will apply that *known* of self,
then there may be given the next step'' (no. 262–69).

There is perhaps no other issue in the modern world about
which we find more confusion than this one of understanding
the nature of our personal responsibilities within the vast
matrix of human circumstances that surrounds us and of
which we are a part. Over long centuries in both East and
West, human thought and related feeling have oscillated between views of freedom and determinism, between wildly
open views of human possibilities and narrowly constricting
perceptions of human limitations with many variations between the two extremes. In particular, our twentieth-century
experience with totalitarian governments of varying ideolo-
gies has led many contemporary pundits of our societies to
conclude that there is no hope for persons placed in con-
stricted politico-economic circumstances except through liberation by external forces. Such has been the doctrine of both
Marxian Communism and National Socialism, and it appears
to be a premise of at least some forms of contemporary liberation theology.

The Edgar Cayce readings differ sharply from this kind of

world-view. They see human life as "under a dispensation of mercy" and urge us to "count thy hardships, thy troubles, even thy disappointments, rather as stepping-stones to know His way better. Be ye happy in *His love*. For He hath loved us, even when afar. How much more when we try, though we may stumble and fail! For the trial, the test, the *determination* creates that which will rise as faithful, true, and as righteousness before the Throne of grace" (no. 262–83).

This perception of the human situation both large and small does not mean that individuals are to accept passively and supinely their circumstances as they find them, without hope of change or without effort on their own part to effect change, both internal and external. Quite the contrary; the Cayce readings repeatedly call for human effort, such as is possible, in every situation. Such admonitions lie in the context of a worldview that posits a divinely structured yet flexibly open order of circumstances. This order allows, indeed it encourages, human effort—however insignificant the effort may appear at any one time and place. The further affirmation is that, under God, such effort is truly effective and will bear good fruit in the long run—and in the short. The readings frequently describe the spiritual growth of human beings in terms of steps to be taken—even in the most untoward circumstances—"day by day, step by step." "As we apply that which we know, we are given the next step," is the phrase in *A Search for God*. In this context of meaning, verses from Isaiah are often quoted or rephrased, "Precept upon precept, precept upon precept, line upon line, line upon line, here a little, there a little" (no. 922–1; no. 3416–1; no. 262–12; compare Isa. 28:10, 13).

This is a vision of human life as an upward climb, a vision much like that of the Apostle Paul when he wrote to the church in Philippi (Greece) toward the end of his life, "I press on toward the goal of the upward call of God in Christ Jesus" (Phil. 3:14). This all is in the context of faith that "the will of the Father [is] that no soul should perish but that there may be the burning of the dross, that it may be sifted as wheat, that it may be purified even as He through suffering in the material things that *are* for the soul's edification'' (no. 262–77; compare 2 Pet. 3:9; 1 Cor. 3:10–15; Luke 22:31—note the plural pronouns in the Greek—Heb. 5:7–10).

This vision of human life, however, is not to be seen as hopeful merely in a grim sense. The Cayce readings tell us to work patiently, to be sure, ''Learn again patience, yet persistent patience, active patience—not merely passive. Patience does not mean merely waiting . . . So with patience, comply with patience's laws, working together with love, purpose, faith, hope, charity'' (no. 1968–5). Yet this patient toil, as the above suggests, is to be undertaken in noble spirit and in the context of high expectancy, ''If the problems of the experience today, now, are taken as an expectancy for the unusual and [for] that which is to be creative and hopeful and helpful, life becomes rather the creative song of the joyous worker'' (no. 1968–5). ''Keep creative ever in the activities. This too. Be *glad* you have the opportunity to be alive at this time, and to be a part of that preparation for the coming influences of a spiritual nature that *must* rule the world. . . . Be happy, happy of it, and give thanks daily for it'' (no. 2376–3). (An intimation of the eschatology of the Cayce readings is also given in this quotation.) A further basis for human hope is given in the following brief description of the structures of human life in this, God's universe, from *A Search for God*: ''In whatever way we prepare ourself, then, the time and place to use that prepared will come.''

Hence the Cayce readings urge, ''Don't be weary in welldoing. If it requires years, give years—but give a service and a praise continually to God, if ye would have life'' (no. 3684–1). We are told to let the Light ''take its time with thee'' (no. 2072–4). Even though we be separated from our loved ones, ''we learn more and more that separations are only walking through the rooms, as it were, of God's house . . .'' (no. 1391–1; compare John 14:2). Physical death is but ''God's other door'' (no. 5749–3). ''For it is not all of life to live, nor all of death to die, for one is the birth of the other, when viewed from the whole or center'' (no. 369–3).

According to the Cayce readings the whole of this human, indeed cosmic, panorama must be seen as supremely in the context of relationship. Though the way be long and sometimes hard, we walk not alone. We are told, ''Ye cannot bear the burden alone, but He has promised—and He is faithful!—'If ye put thy yoke upon me, *I* will guide you' '' (no. 262–77; compare Matt. 11:29–30). ''For, as He hath given, which is the greater promise from the foundation of the world, 'If ye call, I will hear, and answer speedily—though ye be far away, I will hear—I will answer' '' (no. 1747–5; compare Ps. 3:4; 4:3; 6:8–9; 10:17; 18:6; 22:24; 28:6; 31:22, and so on; also Luke 18:8). In *A Search for God* the statement is, ''His abiding presence is in and with us.'' (One of the major contributions of the Cayce readings is to reemphasize the central importance of prayer in human life, as well as to offer fresh modes of practice thereof.) There is no reason even to fear ''the last enemy,'' as the Apostle Paul called death, ''when the trust of the soul and heart of the man is in the Lord, who doeth all things well'' (no. 5195–1; 1 Cor. 15:26). According to P. Franklin Chambers's *Juliana of Norwich*, a similar perception of divine providence in that ''He doeth all things well'' is found in the fourteenth-century English anchoress and mystic.

One or two points need to be added regarding the event of Jesus' raising Lazarus from the dead. Lazarus, as we have noted, is said to have lived after the event ''only until the first of the rebellions arose'' (no. 295–8). Several readings refer to the ''great feast . . . made for Lazarus and the Master with His disciples'' (no. 2791–1); ''The sisters—Martha, Mary—made preparations for the supper, after the resurrection or the bringing to life of the brother'' (no. 1179–2). This is also described as ''the great feast given to the friends and to Jesus and His disciples'' (no. 2787–1). Another reading identifies this event as ''the feast of thanksgiving to those peoples from Jerusalem, as well as Bethany, when the supper was given to Lazarus'' (no. 2519–8; compare John 12:1–12).

There are various references in the readings to the custom then common in Palestine of hiring mourners for funerals. Specific mention is made of such having been hired upon the death of Lazarus (no. 2787–1; no. 3179–1; no. 5148–2). We have already seen that there were those among the disciples of Jesus who took notes and kept records during his public ministry (no. 5148–2). We note also reference to pictorial art (frescoes) in the life of the early church. One reading speaks of those who attempted to ''make or draw upon the walls of the meeting places of some of those groups the activities of that Teacher.'' Apparently ''the first one drawn was the raising of Lazarus'' (no. 2398–2).

11

LATER ENCOUNTERS

THE CAYCE READINGS offer richly suggestive additions to the biblical accounts of the rich young man (called a "ruler" only in Luke 18:18) who was challenged by Jesus regarding his wealth and—only for a time, the readings say—sorrowfully refused to follow the Master's call to discipleship (compare Mark 10:17–31 and parallels). The young man is said to have been a "student of the law, which means a student of the unwritten as well as that interpreted from the penal, the spiritual, and the marital code" (no. 2677–1). This reading is noteworthy as it refers to later and sometimes excessive interpretations of the biblical accounts; for the young man is said to have been "that one about whom much speculation has been in the minds of many—over what is written there in the records, concerning which many a verbose orator has proclaimed much about which he knew so little." The reading goes on to describe

the rich young ruler who declared, "These [commandments] have I kept from my youth up. What lack I yet?" "Sell [Jesus responds] that thou hast, come and follow me." And he went away sorrowing.

But remember another line, "The Master loved the young man" [compare Mark 10:21].

He whom the Master has favored, in mind or in purpose, may count his soul indeed fortunate. Remember one of those eternal laws, "He hath not willed that any soul should perish." (no. 2677–1; compare 1 Tim. 2: 4; 4:10; 2 Pet. 3:9)

This reading then goes on to state that the young man later reconsidered and came to follow Jesus, that he was among those influential in stimulating the Pharisee Nicodemus' quest of the Lord (compare John 3:1–15), and that he contributed to the care of Jesus' body after it was taken down from the cross: "He came, later, and followed. Who prompted Nicodemus to seek the Lord? Who prompted those that cared for the body when it was placed in a new tomb yet unused?" (no. 2677–1; compare Matt. 27:60).

The young man's experience with Jesus, the reading also affirms, became a source in his case particularly of the virtue of tolerance, which "is the basis of patience, and in patience, my son, even as He gave, ye became aware of thy soul and its relationships to the purposes of Infinity with the finite" (compare Luke 21:19). (We may well question the RSV translation of the term "patience" [Greek *hypomone*, Latin *patientia*] in this Lucan passage as "endurance" [also in Rom. 5:3–4 and elsewhere]. For a variety of historical as well as literary reasons, the older King James word patience is to be preferred in this case, as in Luke 17:21 the preferred translation is "within you.") The Cayce readings have much to say of the importance of patience, both as a significant element in the teaching of Jesus and of the apostolic writings and as an indispensable part of a wise and balanced life before God. Indeed patience is cited, along with time and space, as one of the three integral elements in the structure of the cosmos experienced by human beings in the three-dimensional plane (no. 4035–1).

The reading just cited adds that none of the three concepts of "time, space and patience . . . exists in fact, except in the concept of the individual as [he/she] may apply [self] to time or space or patience." The Cayce addition of "patience" to the duality of space and time is particularly interesting in this post-Einstein era of cosmological thought. In the Cayce readings both space and time are held to be human concepts or modes of organizing human perception, but their role is seen as properly fulfilled only when the mental-spiritual attitude and practice of patience are added.

Another reading, in speaking of the rich young man, emphasizes that "Blessed indeed is the entity to whom or about whom it was said, 'As the Master looked on him, He loved him'" (no. 1416–1). This reading gives contemporary advice that may provide insight into the more precise meaning that Jesus intended with his original call. The reading urges the person who requested it to "hold fast to that thou hast heard" and specifically affirms the rightness of following the commandments that the rich young ruler had indeed faithfully followed. It then says, "Give that thou hast—not all of thy worldly goods, but that thou hast attained, by bringing hope and help in the experiences of those who have lost their perspective, who have lost their way." (This pair of readings given for two different persons offers a discrepancy that is only rarely seen in the entire corpus of Cayce readings. One (no. 1416) was a thirty-four-year-old man when his reading was given in 1937. The other man (no. 2677) was twenty-one when his reading was given in 1942. Each of these men was identified as having been the rich young man of the gospel accounts. This apparent mistake in the information, or contradiction, was not explained.)

This suggestion for contemporary application seems to mean that the giving of material wealth to others is only one part—perhaps a less important part—of the service of others to which Jesus calls his disciples. We may recall that only in Luke is the ruler directed to sell all that he has and distribute to the poor (Luke 18:22). In Matthew we read Jesus' saying, "If you would be perfect, go, sell what you possess and give to the poor" (Matt. 19:21). Mark merely has, "go, sell what you have, and give to the

poor'' (Mark 10:21). The Lucan language at this point is in
keeping with the author's phraseology in other passages
(compare Acts 2:44–45).

A final point, however, should be added. Another reading
affirms that in the original case the problem for the young
man was not so much craving for luxury, or for wealth as
such, as it was fear of lack: "He [Jesus] wept with the young
man who turned away. . . . He was sorry for the young man
. . . the fear of lack, the fear of the lack of the medium of
exchange—or of wealth—hindered'' (no. 2533–7).

BARTIMAEUS

We find in the Cayce readings several references to the blind
beggar Bartimaeus, whose sight was restored by Jesus at Jericho, a town on the banks of the river Jordan (compare Mark
10:46–52 and parallels). Two readings speak of Bartimaeus
as having been a physically strong man, who lost his sight
while working at his craft as a metal worker (no. 2124–3;
no. 688–2).

Although the New Testament gives us no information
about Bartimaeus after his healing, the readings emphasize
that his services and their influence among his contemporaries were indeed great. In particular he sought to "bring the
awakening of the inner man, to the abilities of that contact
as may be made by the calling *on* His [the Christ's] name"
(no. 2124–3). Originally driven to begging by reason of his
blindness, Bartimaeus's response to his healing was point-
edly that of one now "mindful that those so aided are not
. . . spongers upon the good graces of those that would aid"
(no. 2124–3; see also no. 5277–1). In other words Bartimaeus believed that he was healed of physical blindness so
that he might become a fully responsible person in his society.

In one of the readings related to Bartimaeus we find a brief
description of the movement focusing on Jesus of Nazareth

as "a cause that reached into and awakened all those promises [of God] that have been set from the beginning" (no. 688–2). This is another way of stating that in Jesus the Christ we find the recapitulation as well as the fulfillment of all that had historically occurred in the experience of humanity within the economy of God. In this same reading we find a high Christology that affirms, in the context of the Cayce readings' understanding of and emphasis upon the cosmic Christ, the wider work of God in the world, the indispensability of the role of the Christ in every authentic spiritual activity in human history.

I sum up this Cayce perception elsewhere with the statement that every person in every place has ongoing access to spiritual channels that may be used and blessed by the Spirit of the Christ, by the Holy Spirit, the universal Spirit of the Father, whether these channels bear the name Christian or not. In the case of this reading, the universal divine presence and work is placed in the context of Jesus' affirmation of his return to the Father, from which "place" of work his saving, helping, guiding, protecting relationship may be made available to all, ". . . as He has given, 'I go to prepare the place, that where I am there ye may be also' " (no. 688–2; compare John 14:2–3).

In this context of understanding, then, we read, "Only in Him may the cleansing come . . . for His name is above *every* name, for through that name thou may approach the Throne of grace itself" (no. 688–2; compare Phil. 2:9–10). In this reading something of the meaning of Bartimaeus's experience of suffering during his period of blindness is intimated with the statement that he learned "the ability to suffer in body that the soul might be made alive in Him." In another reading brief mention is made of Jesus' healing the son of the Roman governor Pontius Pilate after his healing of Bartimaeus (no. 324–5; compare Matt. 27:19).

In the Bartimaeus readings we find further material on the teaching of Jesus with regard to the proper relation of self to God and others. Using the term self here in the sense of selfishness, a reading says that much may be done "if self is put entirely aside" (no. 5277–1; compare Matt. 10:38–39; 16:24–25; Mark 8:34–35; John 12:25). In the Cayce readings one definition of sin is plain selfishness, especially in the sense of self-centeredness (compare no. 262–29; 262–64). Indeed it is selfishness that makes us afraid (no. 262–29) and hence self in this sense, even though it may be "the most interesting thing in life, . . . yet self must become null and void, as *losing* self *in* love for another (no. 262–2); compare Matt. 10:38–39 and parallels). But the self as such, as the *locus* of the self-awareness given us by our Maker and thereby constituting our reality—our soul—as the image of God, is of course not to be annihilated.

The language of losing is metaphorical. And in the Cayce readings the self is never said to be evil in itself, however it may be evilly misused by self. Indeed the readings insist repeatedly that in a primary sense—not solely, but in a primary sense—we meet God, or the risen Christ, within. "The lesson of the Teacher, the Christ, the Master is to look within self." This is in part to know oneself and supremely one's need of conscious relationship with one's Maker, " 'For of myself I can do *nothing*,' but it is the God that worketh within thee!" (no. 688–4; compare John 5:19; 1 Cor. 4:16–17; 6:15, 19; 2 Cor. 6:16). (It should be noted again in this context that the Cayce readings emphasize in the strongest way that the kingdom of God is within, as in the Greek text of Luke 17:20–21. For example we read, "The consciousness of His abiding presence is within, even as He gave, 'The kingdom of God is also without' [compare 262–28]; this is the reality that is also sometimes termed the kingdom of the Father" [no. 262–27].) At the same time we are told, "I [the Christ] will meet thee in thine own activities toward thy fellow man" (no. 688–2). This is to say that our meeting the Master "within" is properly an event not only interior in what is called religious experience, that is, in prayer and meditation, in vision and dream, but also a fellowship to be exercised in the midst of activities related to our fellow human beings.

These Bartimaeus readings also stress that in our relationship to others our persistent posture should be that of "not condemning any, for thine own self would condemn thee. Dost thou make for self's own aggrandizement through those relationships in this or that with thine fellow man, thou hast thine reward—and so must meet that thou sowest" (no. 688–2; compare Matt. 6:1–4, 16–18; 7:1–2). This principle of sowing and reaping is of course a principle basic to the teaching of the entire Bible, Old Testament as well as New; it is as central in the apostolic writings as in the teachings of Jesus (compare Matt. 7:2, 21; 10:26; 16:27; Luke 12:47–48; John 5:14; 8:34; Acts 24:25; Rom. 2:6; 2 Cor. 5:10; 9:6, 10; Gal. 5:15; 6:7; Eph. 6:8; Col. 3:25; 2 Thess. 1:6; Jas. 1:13; 3:16; 5:4; 1 Pet. 1:17; 3:12; 2 Pet. 2:13, 16; Rev. 2:23; 14:8, 13; 18:6; 20:12, 13; 22:12).

This principle of meeting again in the economy of God that which one has sown is a truth frequently affirmed in the Cayce readings, even to the extent—in conformity with Jesus' own strong statement in Matthew 12:36—that "Thou must meet every word thou hast uttered in thine experience" (no. 688–2). We shall consider later in more detail *how* we are to meet ourselves and the consequences of self's doing-being. At this point, let us note simply that we best meet them "in Him," in the context of fellowship with the living God, by dependence upon his love and mercy, his cleansing and healing power. As stated in *A Search for God*, "No soul has been left without access to the throne of mercy and grace."

In the Bartimaeus readings there is a theme that is also strongly emphasized in the New Testament: humility, a theme that is not very popular in most industrialized countries of the modern world. One reading takes up this theme first with advice to "Hold fast to that love that He gave, and ye will find peace and harmony, much strength and much power" (no. 688–4). Then further word is given to indicate that humility is needed for these results to be obtained, for the "love that He gave" is manifested "only in *humbling* of self and self's own emotions, self's own self!" The woman who is said to have been the mother of Bartimaeus is told, "In the application in the present, then, mind not high things; condescend rather to things of low estate. Humble thyself as one to another, as ye did through those experiences, and so manifest in Him—how that the King even of kings suffered with those that would betray even his fellow man" (no. 688–4; compare Rom. 12:16; Phil. 2:1–11; Mark 14:10–72). In this context sharp, perhaps severe, warning is added: "If credit is taken here, or if it is sought that others thank thee or bless thee or praise thee for the efforts that ye put forth, then ye are seeking *self*-glory; the ego of self is seeking expression!" (no. 688–4).

Another reading discusses the theme of humility in connection with Jesus' teaching: " 'He that is greatest among you will be the servant of all.' Learn, then, *humbleness* and *believe*" (no. 1265–2; compare Mark 10:43 and parallels). This reading goes on to give the following as specific application of the principle, "until each entity may see in the individual who is as his enemy, as that one he dislikes or whose ways he dislikes, such as is the image [*imago Dei*] of that he would worship in the Father, he may not in deed and in truth know the way."

A few brief statements are made in the Cayce readings about the conversion of the tax collector Zacchaeus, an event that also occurred in Jericho but is recorded in the New Testament only in the Gospel of Luke (19:1–10). The fact that "Zacchaeus was called from the tree" and that a "feast [was] made by Zacchaeus for the Master and His disciples" is duly noted (no. 3377–1). The "enthusiasm of Zacchaeus" is cited as if it were somewhat excessive and not accompanied as yet with adequate understanding. Yet even though Zacchaeus's response in some ways exceeded proper bounds, with loving patience "that day the Lord supped with him" (no. 254–54). Another reading gives in a few striking words intimation of the deeper meaning of the event: "Zacchaeus climbed higher that he might have the broader vision, and that day dined with Truth" (no. 307–4).

Part III

THE END AND
THE BEGINNING

12

THE LAST WEEK

FOR THE WRITERS of the New Testament gospels, the events of the last week of Jesus' earthly life clearly constitute the climax of that life and play a commanding role in the whole. The Cayce readings are in no wise different. We may properly begin their accounts with a statement about the prelude to the events:

> In those days preceding the entry into Jerusalem, we find those periods of much disturbance among the disciples who were of Galilee and those who were of the Jerusalem ministry. These were in disputations as to what was to take place when He, Jesus, was to go to Jerusalem [compare Mark 8:31–33; 10:32–34 and parallels].
>
> Yet He chose to go, entering through the period of rest at Bethany with Mary, Martha, Lazarus; and *there* [Jerusalem] the triumphal entry and the message that was given to those throngs gathered there. (no. 5749–10; compare Mark 11:1–11 and parallels)

The distinction between Jesus' disciples of Galilean and Judean background, here mentioned with concomitant differences in outlook, is a cultural reality easily imaginable but only to be inferred from the New Testament gospels. The first three or synoptic gospels, apart from the events of the last week, focus on the Galilean ministry of Jesus. Only the gospel of John gives us a somewhat different picture by indicating that Jesus made at least three trips to Jerusalem to celebrate the Passover during his public ministry (John 2:23; 6:4; 11:55); and, if the unnamed feast mentioned in John 5: 1 was a Passover festival, four. In terms of chronology the Fourth Gospel places the cleansing of the temple at the beginning of Jesus' ministry rather than at the end (compare John 2:13–22; Mark 11:15–19 and parallels). The Gospel of John also identifies and gives us fuller details about such Judean disciples such as Nicodemus, Martha, Mary, Lazarus, and Joseph of Arimathea (compare John 3:1–15; 9:1–41; 11: 1–12, 19; 19:38–42; 20:1–18). In fact the Cayce readings as a whole tend to follow the Johannine tradition more than the synoptic, both biographically and theologically.

The decision of Jesus to go to Jerusalem for what became the last week of his earthly ministry is described in another reading that may constitute an extracanonical saying of the Lord: "When He gave, 'I must go up that I may be offered as the living sacrifice' " (no. 897–1). This statement, if authentic, is in essential conformity with the Marcan account of the "intention" of Jesus (compare Mark 10:45; 1 Tim. 2: 5–6).

We read also that at this time immediately preceding the Passover celebration "there was the gatherings [in Jerusalem] of those from many lands . . ." (no. 681–1), including "all the lands nigh unto the Galilean, the Phoenician or Syrophoenician, Tyre, and Sidon [from which] . . . all the peoples had come as *one* for the days that were counted as holy" (no. 1301–1). We read elsewhere that people came from afar to Jerusalem not only for the purpose of worship but also "for the social and companionable activities during such feasts" (no. 1456–1).

As we have seen, the Cayce readings at many points stress the international relationships and activities of at least part of the spectrum of Jewish religious parties or schools at the time of Jesus, especially of the Essenes. Presumably these persons were all Jewish in some sense, that is, fully ethnic Jews, proselytes, or at least Gentile "worshipers of God"— to use the terminology and categories of the Acts of the Apostles. According to the readings, however, many had heard of Jesus—some from his visit(s) to Tyre and Sidon— and there were differences of opinion among them, as among Palestinian Jews, as to whether "there was to be either the establishing of the material kingdom by that man, or there were to be [focus on] the understandings of what those teachings were to bring into the experience of others" (no. 681–1). The reference here would seem to point to differences in interpretation and expectation as to whether the primary purpose and meaning of Jesus' ministry were political, religious, or some combination of the two.

One reading that uses the phrase "the triumphal entry into the city" comments, with regard to "the crowd of people" who welcomed Jesus, that "though man would have us believe that there were great throngs, they were mostly women and children"—a statement gently critical of the gospel accounts but quite believable on the basis of our human experience, historical and contemporary (no. 3615–1; compare Mark 11:1–10 and parallels; also see Luke 8:1–3). Another reading states that "the ass, upon which the Master rode, was . . . a physical manifestation of kingship, of lordship" (no. 5257–1). This interpretation of the meaning of the event is in accord with the understanding of the Gospels of Matthew and John, following the Hebrew prophet Zechariah (compare Matt. 21:1–11; John 12:12–15; Zech. 9:9). The quotation from Zechariah is not found in Mark or Luke.

This latter reading briefly refers to the singular effect of "the light of the eyes of the Master" (no. 5257–1). Another also speaks of "the eyes of the Master as He passed by on the road or the way to the city on that day of days" (no. 1301–1). This was the time "when He gave that if it were not for the cry of the peoples the very hills and mountains would cry out, 'Hosanna, Glory in the Highest'—for the

Prince of Peace comes to make those decisions whereunto
man again has his closer, *closer* associations with his
Maker . . .'' (no. 1301–1; compare Mark 11:9–10 and parallels; see also 2 Cor. 5:17–21). This last statement gives us
in brief expression the Cayce readings' understanding of the
primary purpose of Jesus' life and ministry—supremely of
his death on the cross, his resurrection and ascension—as the
reconciliation of persons, the restoration and healing of personal relationships, first with our Maker, then with each
other, indeed with the whole of creation.

Reading no. 1301–1 also gives a suggestive interpretation
of a statement of Jesus recorded in the Gospel of John, in
which Jesus, quoting Psalm 82:6, affirms the truth of the
psalmist's phrase, ''You are gods . . . to whom the word of
God came'' (John 10:34–36). The Cayce reading at this point
states in interpretation ''that man as man may be far from
God, but man as a god and acting godly may be close to the
divine'' (no. 1301–1). This is, of course, to change the intent
of the discourse from primary concern with questions of on-
tology to issues ethical and relational. The entire corpus of
the Cayce readings, however, seems to be one in their anthropological understanding, seeing every human being as
the *imago Dei*, created in essence, as soul, in the image of
God (no. 1265–2, A-1; compare Gen 1:26–27; 5:1).

Another reading describes the scene of the triumphal entry
as follows:

Even as He gave on that memorable day . . . if the people had not cried 'Hosanna!'—the very rocks, the very
trees, the very nature about, would cry out *against*
those opportunities lost by the children of men, [op-
portunities] to proclaim the great day of the Lord! . . .
[For this was] He that brought hope and cheer to those
that were ill in body, those that had lost hope through
the holding to material things and to the old tenets of
tradition. (no. 1468–1)

Following these words that speak as aptly and hopefully to our modern situation as to the ancient, the reading goes to indicate how the crowds included people of every class and condition, telling of "the great throng as they spread their garments—yea, those of high and low estate or position," even though, as we have seen, most were women and children.

THE LAST SUPPER

The Last Supper is specifically cited in the Cayce readings as "the passover—which He kept with His disciples" and as "the last supper with His beloved disciples" (no. 2794–3). One reading in particular gives us an astonishingly detailed picture of the event. This account was not asked for but was given voluntarily by the sleeping Cayce at the end of another reading (no. 1315–3), even though the suggestion to wake up had been given him three times.

> The Lord's Supper—here with the Master—see what they had for supper, boiled fish, rice, with leeks, wine, and loaf. One of the pitchers in which it was served was broken—the handle was broken, as was the lip to same.
>
> The whole robe of the Master was not white, but pearl gray—all combined into one [compare John 19: 23]—the gift of Nicodemus to the Lord.
>
> The better looking of the twelve, of course, was Judas, while the younger was John—oval face, dark hair, smooth face—only one with short hair. Peter, the rough and ready—always that of very short beard, rough and not altogether clean; while Andrew's is just the opposite—very sparse, but inclined to be long more on the side and under the chin—long on the upper lip—his robe was always near gray or black, while his

clouts or breeches were striped; while those of Philip and Bartholomew were red and brown.

The Master's hair is 'most red, inclined to be curly in portions, yet not feminine or weak—*strong*, with heavy piercing eyes that are blue or steel-gray.

His weight would be at least a hundred and seventy pounds. Long, tapering fingers, nails well kept. Long nail, though, on the left little finger.

Merry—even in the hour of trial. Joke—even in the moment of betrayal.

The sack is empty. Judas departs.

The last is given of the wine and loaf, with which He gives the emblems that should be so dear to every follower of Him. Lays aside His robe, which is all of one piece, girds the towel about His waist, which is dressed in linen that is blue and white. Rolls back the folds, kneels first before John, James, then to Peter— who refuses [compare John 13:3–11].

Then the dissertation as to "He that would be the greatest would be the servant of all."

The basin is taken as without handle, and is made of wood. The water is from the gherkins [gourds] that are in the wide-mouth shibboleths [large water jars], that stand in the house of John's father, Zebedee.

And now comes, "It is finished."

They sing the ninety-first Psalm—"He that dwelleth in the secret place of the Most High shall abide under the shadow of the Almighty.

I will say of the Lord, He is my refuge and my fortress, my God, in Him will I trust."

He is the musician as well, for He uses the harp.

They leave for the garden. (no. 5749–1; compare Mark 14:12–31 and parallels)

It is interesting that, while the first day of the feast of un-leavened bread is described in the New Testament as the time "when they sacrificed the passover lamb" (Mark 14:12 and parallels), nowhere in the scriptural accounts is it stated that Jesus and his disciples actually ate lamb at the supper.

In regard to Jesus' teaching, "He that would be the greatest would be the servant of all," the reading is in agreement with the Gospels of Luke and John (Luke 22:26–27; John 13:12–17), which, differently from Mark and Matthew (Mark 10:43–44; Matt. 23:11–12), assign this teaching to the occasion of the Last Supper. Another reading agrees in the following context: "That faith, that hope that brings into the present experience a *joy* in being of a service to others—from that lesson as gained then from the words He spoke at the Last Supper, 'He that would be the greatest among you will be the minister, the servant, serving others' " (no. 2778–2).

The New Testament record of Jesus' statement "It is finished" cites it as one of his words spoken while hanging on the cross (John 19:30; compare John 4:34; 17:4).

In another reading we find a reference to the Last Supper that emphasizes the meaning of Jesus' washing his disciples' feet

> in the upper chamber with the disciples, and the humbleness that was manifested.
>
> Though He was their leader, their prophet, their Lord, their Master, He signified—through the humbleness of the act—the attitude to which each would come, if he would know that true relationship with his God, his fellowman. (no. 5749–10; compare John 13:1–20)

Jesus' inauguration of the Lord's Supper as an abiding rite to be performed by his followers, a rite that would be part of their acts of public worship, is briefly noted in the words "the establishing of the emblems as His body and blood, as a ritual for those who would honor and bring to remembrance those experiences through which each soul passes in putting on the whole armor of the Christ" (no. 5749–10; compare Luke 22:19 RSV footnote; Eph. 6:11, 13; Rom. 13:12).

(Reading no. 3615–1 describes this part of the Last Supper experience as follows: "in the hour that there was set forth the emblem of the broken body and the shed blood, in order that man might ever be mindful of same.") The quote from reading 5749–10 gives us, in perhaps surprising mode for the context, the familiar emphasis of the Cayce readings upon the necessity to practice in daily life the tenets and rituals of faith. It is also another statement of the affirmation frequently found that, although the scale and "order" of things be different in some degree, the events and experiences of the life of Jesus the Christ constitute the true and right pattern for the life of every human being.

Another reading seems to affirm the "Real Presence" in the sacrament of the Lord's Supper, "And in the breaking of bread ye may know Him!" (no. 1158–9). The larger context of this reading affirms the ongoing presence of the risen Christ in various modes of human experience. "Thou hast seen Him oft in the acts of others and the personality ye called by another name, yet ye may see Him. And when He speaks, 'Be not afraid, it is I,' know He is near. And in the breaking of bread ye may know Him" (no. 1158–9; compare Matt. 25:31–46). It is of course also possible to interpret this last sentence as indicating the potential presence of the risen Lord in every event of human table fellowship.

Then again, as frequently found in the Cayce readings, the role of human cooperation in the relational process is emphasized. "He that would know his own way, his own relationships to Creative Forces or God may seek through the promises in Him—as set in Jesus of Nazareth—He passeth by! Will ye have Him enter and sup with thee? *Open* then thy heart, thy consciousness, for He would tarry with thee!" (no. 5755–1).

Frequent mention is made, in a variety of contexts, of the fourteenth, fifteenth, sixteenth, and seventeenth chapters of the Gospel of John as constituting the heart of the Christian Gospel, the essence of Jesus' teaching, and the very section of the Judeo-Christian Scriptures that those who wish to grow in faith, understanding, and obedience should especially and frequently read. "Read then the fourteenth, fifteenth, sixteenth, and seventeenth of John. And reading it, not as rote, ye will find that even He is speaking, even as to thee!" (no. 1010–12). Directions such as this are found not only in readings where information was specifically requested about the life and teaching of Jesus, but are scattered widely across the whole corpus of readings and addressed to many persons. It is worthy of note that the well-known Indian Christian evangelist and mystic of the earlier part of this century, Sundar Singh, placed comparable emphasis upon the Gospel of John both for its intrinsic meaning and value theologically and for its importance in his own devotional life.

We find in the readings statements that the apostle John frequently related to Mary the mother of Jesus, "and the other Mary" (no. 2946–3), the events and words "of the last hours of the Master" (no. 2946–2). This last phrase refers not only to "those pronouncements made upon the cross . . . [and] the last hour in the garden, on the way to the garden" (2946–3), but also to the Last Supper, for to these women

these [words] have a special meaning: "Let not your heart to be troubled—ye believe in God, believe also in me; for in my Father's house are many mansions. If it were not so, I would have told you. I go to prepare a place for you, that where I am there ye maybe also. The *way* ye know." He, then, is indeed the Way, the Truth, the Light. (no. 2946–3; compare John 14:1–6)

A significant rephrasing of these words—quite in keeping with Cayce themes—is found in another reading. "Were it not so, I would have told you. I prepare a place for those that are faithful, are patient, that they—too—may be with me as from the foundations of the earth" (no. 1158–5).

Frequent mention is made in the readings of the following Johannine quotation of Jesus' words, "as He hath given, 'If ye love me ye will keep my commandments, and my commandments are not grievous—only that ye love one another' '' (no. 2620–2; compare John 14:15; 1 John 5:3). Frequent reference is also made to what is recorded in John 14:26 RSV as the role of ''the Counselor, the Holy Spirit, whom the Father will send in my name, he will teach you all things, and bring to your remembrance all that I have said to you.'' This saying is found with varying phraseology but almost always with a somewhat widened perspective, such as, ''I will bring to thee remembrance of all that is necessary for thine understanding from the foundations of the earth, if ye will but keep my commandments'' (no. 518–1).

Perceptive readers will no doubt discern from the above that the Cayce readings take with the utmost seriousness as veritable *ipsis-sima verba* of Jesus the longer account of the experience of the Last Supper as given in the Gospel of John. Indeed, as we have already noted, the faith perspective of the Edgar Cayce readings is generally closer to the Johannine record than to that of the other gospel writers—in so far as there may be difference of record or of interpretation.

JUDAS ISCARIOT

With regard to Judas's betrayal of Jesus, which in one sense comes to a focus at the time of the Last Supper, we find the following question and answer given in a reading,

Q-27. Was Judas Iscariot's idea in betraying Jesus to force Him to assert Himself as a king and bring in His kingdom then?

A-27. Rather the desire of the man to force same, and the fulfilling of that as Jesus spoke of same at the supper. (no. 2067–7; compare Mark 14:17–21, and parallels)

The Cayce readings insist that Judas was a free agent in the entire series of events, "For did He not commit the keeping of the worldly goods to Judas [compare John 12:4–6; 13:29]? Did He not give to him the power, the opportunity to meet himself?" (no. 1265–2). This last sentence is of course to include Judas in the same context of divinely providential ordering—open-ended, open-hearted—that the readings see as set for every human being.

In this same reading, which was given for a person who believed himself to have been Judas Iscariot in a former incarnation (a mistaken belief, according to the reading), the statement is made that there was a Jewish "cult" at the time that had foretold that Judas would betray his Lord and commit other crimes. Therefore it was noted with special interest by some at the beginning of Jesus' public ministry that Judas had been "accepted by one that others proclaimed as a teacher, a master." The reading, however, goes on to emphasize—even though it was not addressed to Judas—that no one is to despair, not even Judas! (no. 1265–2; compare no. 137–125).

> For know within that the Master, the Lord thy God, overlooks that thou hast done and has given, "Whosoever will may take the cup . . ." Know, He hath willed that each soul should know the way, and hath prepared a way. Then look not back upon the associations, those environmental forces, nor thine own curiosity, but rather look up—to Him who may call thee that thou may know and see His face! (no. 1265–2; compare John 14:4–6)

GETHSEMANE

The Cayce readings lay singular weight upon Jesus' inner experience in the garden of Gethsemane. This time is seen as among the most critical decision-events in Jesus' public ministry, as a time of climax and also one inwardly most painful. "Those periods in the garden—these becoming that in which great trial is shown, and the seeming indifference [of his disciples] and the feeling of the loss of one in whom trust and hope had been given; and the fulfilling of all that had been in the purpose and the desire in the entrance into the world" (no. 5749–10; compare Mark 14:32–52 and parallels). Thus the readings state that Jesus' selection of Judas was sincere and the latter's defection and betrayal a matter of genuinely free choice, not an automatic fulfillment of prophecy seen as cosmically determined.

We note also that "the real test was in the garden . . . in the realization that He had met every test and yet must know the pang of death" (no. 5777–1). Another reading states that "He sighed with the very blood of His body in Gethsemane" (no. 1158–5). We may infer therefore that the readings seem to include the whole of the last week, indeed the whole life of Jesus, as, in one sense, part of his "passion."

Quite another dimension, however, is added to these experiences by a reading in which the person addressed is told, "See the funny side [of life]—don't be too serious. Remember, He even made the joke as He walked to the garden to be betrayed. Remember, He looked with love upon His disciple that denied Him, even as He stood alone" (no. 2448–2).

Another reading states, "The smile is as that look which the Master gave Peter, and he went out and wept—for he found himself" (no. 3578–1; compare Luke 22:61; Matt. 10:39). This perception of the humor of Jesus, of his compassionate and hope-filled smile, even at the most critical or perilous moments of his life, is one of the most significant original contributions of the Cayce readings to the understanding of the person and work of Jesus.

It is also said, in another reading, of Jesus on the way to the cross, "remember—He laughed even on the way to Calvary; not as pictured so oft, but laughed even at those that tormented Him. This is what angered them the most" (no.

3003–1). There are clear intimations in the New Testament gospels that Jesus maintained a high personal dignity, also a certain surety, together with personal compassion for others, during the events of this last week (Mark 14:9, 25, 62; Luke 23:28–31, 39–43). The possibility, however, that this all was capped by compassionate humor is indeed a rich insight.

In the Cayce readings only a few details are given of the trial of Jesus before the Sanhedrin or of his appearance before the Roman governor (procurator) Pontius Pilate. We have already noted that Jesus had healed Pilate's son (no. 1207–1; 1151–10), and we read elsewhere that Pilate's wife suffered in her position as his wife (no. 764–1; compare Matt. 27:19). It was she who had been persuaded by one in her own household "to seek help in those periods just before the time of the crucifixion" (no. 2513–1). Her son, we are told, had suffered from epilepsy (no. 1754), and in the company of a Roman soldier of Pilate's personal bodyguard she "brought their afflicted or epileptic son to the Master" (1217–1).

The readings relate that following the crucifixion of Jesus a report was made to the Roman emperor Tiberius that was largely favorable to the Christian community of faith and that, as a result, Pilate was recalled to Rome "and one closer in association or in sympathy with the Christian movement . . . appointed in the stead—as is seen or recorded by profane history as well as by intimation in sacred history" (no. 1151–10; see also no. 1158–4, no. 3006–1, and no. 2021–1). Pilate is said to have been personally questioned "by Caesar as related to those things which had come about" (no. 877–27).

From historical sources, primarily Josephus and Philo, we learn that as a result of a succession of arbitrary acts Pilate was ordered to return to Rome to stand trial himself. According to Philo's *De Legatione ad Gaium*, Pilate was described in a letter from Herod Agrippa I, the brother of Herodias and nephew of Herod Antipas (compare Luke 13: 1; 23:12), to the Roman emperor Gaius Caligula as inflexible, merciless, and corrupt. He was in particular accused of executing persons without proper trial.

The Cayce readings say that at the time of Jesus' appearance before Pilate there could be perceived on the face of the Master "that tenderness with which He felt and experienced His aloneness when deserted by those who had been close to Him" (no. 2620–2). During this succession of events, however, Jesus is said to have told a sympathetic woman who had friends among the temple guards, "Be not afraid, for me nor for thyself. All is *well* with thee" (no. 2620–2). Reference is made also to "the unjustness of His trial, the persecutions of His body, that [yet] made the way for mankind, ye His brethen, ye thy own self, to *have* and know the way that leads to 'That peace I leave with thee; not as the world knoweth peace, but my peace I give' " (no. 1504–1; compare I Pet. 2:24; John 14:27).

Not only Pilate, however, is held responsible for Jesus' death. We read also of the role "of the high priest in the condemning" (no. 332–2). The "priest who first condemned the Master" before the Sanhedrin is said to have been a son-in-law of the high priest Caiaphas (no. 2934–1). The Cayce readings, however, while fully acknowledging the physical dimensions of Jesus' suffering in the garden of Gethsemane, at the trial, and on the cross itself, tend to focus on the meaning of the whole and at the same time to suggest that there were certain qualifying or compensatory factors at work. This is to say that the readings do not see the physical and mental suffering of Jesus as one totally unrelieved experience of agony. Jesus' perception of the cosmic significance of his suffering made also for an awareness of the "glory" of the experience. Thus, we read,

> The trial—this was not with the pangs of pain as so oft indicated, but rather glorying in the opportunity of taking upon self that which would *right* man's relationship to the Father—in that man, through his free will, had brought sin into the activities of the children

of God. Here *His Son* was bringing redemption through the shedding of blood that they might be free. (no. 5749–10; compare Mark 10:45; 2 Cor. 5:18–21; Eph. 1:7)

This is to say that the passion of Jesus the Christ—with its climax in his suffering on the cross—was cosmically redemptive (liberating, restoring to right relationships, healing) in the deepest and widest sense of the word: "He gave Himself as a ransom for all" (no. 5749–10; compare Mark 10:45; Matt. 20:38; 1 Tim. 2:6). But this event-series is portrayed in the Cayce readings as occurring in the context of Jesus' personal awareness in the manner of that given in the New Testament Letter to the Hebrews, "Jesus the pioneer and perfecter of our faith, who for the joy that was set before him endured the cross, despising the shame, and is seated at the right hand of the throne of God" (Heb. 12:2).

Another reading, in speaking of "the King on the cross," wonders who of all who were in the city of Jerusalem at that time "thought or felt that there would come the day when His words, even 'My peace I give unto you,' would change the whole world, and that *time*, even, would be counted from that death, that birth" (no. 262–71; compare John 14:27).

In the same 5749 series of readings emphasis is laid upon another theme of the book of Hebrews. In answer to a request for an explanation of the phrase in the Gospel of John 19:34, "forthwith came out blood and water," a phrase appearing in the RSV version as "one of the soldiers pierced his side with a spear, and at once there came out blood and water," a reading says that this is "the fulfilling of 'without the shedding of blood there is no remission of sins.' Hence His blood was shed as the sacrifice of the just for the unjust that ye all may stand in the same light with the Father" (no. 5749–10; Heb. 9:22; compare Rom. 5:15–21).

The Edgar Cayce readings, here as elsewhere, follow directly in the tradition of the New Testament in their perception of the passion of Jesus the Christ, together with his

resurrection and ascension, as bearing a vicarious or substitutionary efficacy in the widest, most inclusive sense of the
word. This is to say that it was, and is, for others (compare
Mark 10:45; Matt. 20:28; 1 Tim. 2:5–6). They are equally
concerned, however, to stress that the effects of this great,
cosmically significant work are not properly to be confined
to the future, or to other realms (as to "heaven"). The redemptive work of Jesus is to be personally and presently
applied in an ongoing and developing way in the everyday
lives of all who look to him as Lord and Savior. Thus, precisely where we read "He gave Himself as a ransom for all,"
we find that this grandly cosmic activity is for the sake of
our "becoming indeed brethren with Him . . . that whoever
will may take their cross and *through* Him know the joy of
entering into that realm of replacing jealousy and hate and
selfishness with love and with joy and with gladness" (no.
5749–10; compare Mark 8:34–35 and parallels).

Further practical application is seen in the admonition that
follows the quotation above. "Be ye glad. Be ye joyous
when those things come to be thy lot that should or would
disturb the material-minded. Like Him, look up, lift up thy
heart, thy mind unto the Giver of all good and perfect gifts,
and cry aloud even as He, 'My God, My God! Be Thou near
me' " (no. 5749–10; compare Luke 21:28; Jas. 1:17; 3:17).

This last quotation should not be understood as though the
Cayce readings do not take seriously the pathos in Jesus' cry
from the cross, " 'Eloi, Eloi, lama sabachthani?' which
means, 'My God, my God, why hast thou forsaken me?' "
(Mark 15:34 and parallels). For we read of "that day when
the sun was darkened and the cry went out to the world, 'My
Lord, my God, why hast thou forsaken me?' " (no. 1929–1;
compare Mark 15:33 and parallels). Elsewhere we read thus
of the death of Jesus, "Not only was He dead in body, but
the soul was separated from that body. As all phases of man
in the earth are made manifest, the physical body, the mental
body, the soul body became as each dependent upon their
own experience. Is it any wonder that the man cried, 'My

God, my God, *why* hast thou forsaken me?' '' (no. 5749–6). The pathos of this cry of Jesus, according to the Cayce readings, is not lightly to be interpreted as merely the opening words of Psalm 22 with its strong conclusions of faith and praise. The depths of the mystery of Jesus' cry upon the cross, however, are not given us, to my knowledge, beyond what we have here.

The cosmic victory won by Jesus in and through his passion, resurrection, and ascension was also a victory for and in himself. The efforts were not only later and for others but also in the person of Jesus. This is the reason why the Cayce readings offer a present application of the "finished work" of Jesus the Christ in saying, "In those periods of transition from 'It is finished' comes that which is to each heart the determination that it, too, may know the blessed hope that comes in seeing, knowing, experiencing the cross in the heart, the body, the mind" (no. 5749–10, compare John 19: 30; Mark 8:34–35 and parallels). That is, we ourselves may know a blessed hope in the very act of experiencing the multidimensional sufferings of our own crosses, because Jesus himself did just that, and perfectly.

The Cayce materials, in this context, quote what may be an extra-canonical word of Jesus, "Be ye joyous in the service of the Lord" (no. 518–1). Indeed the readings speak frequently of "the joys, the *pleasures* in services" (no. 262–3; no. 262–33, and so on). Service is also frequently defined in the following terms: "the greatest service that may be done is the little word here and there, the kindly thought, the little deeds that make the heart glad, and the brightness of the Son come in the lives of all" (no. 262–13; compare no. 262:33). The Cayce readings in this and in almost every other way possible repeatedly emphasize the importance before God, and in cosmic consequence, of the so-called "little things" of human life, the apparently insignificant little words, deeds, and attitudes of ordinary people in everyday living. Hence we are told, "In thine ministry, then [here addressed to "lay" persons], see that each line, each thought is a *practical* thing, *living*, having its being in Him." Indeed the whole work of Edgar Cayce and his associates is described as "practical religion in action" (no. 262–3; compare Matt. 12: 36–37).

We find, therefore, a continued alternation, or reciprocal action, in the Cayce readings between Jesus' suffering and his hope and joy, between our crosses and our hope and joy. His victory at that point of human history—perfect and completed—made possible, we are told, our present appropriation and application—even if imperfect and developing. It is in this context of understanding that we read,

> His heart ached, yea, His body was sore and weary; yea, His body bled not only from the nail prints in His hands and feet but from the spear thrust into the heart of hearts! For the blood as of the perfect man was shed, not by reason of Himself but that there might be made an offering once for all. (no. 1504–1; compare Heb. 9: 26–28; also Matt. 20:28; 26:28; Mark 10:45; I Tim 2: 5–6; Tit. 2:14; I Pet. 1:18–21)

In the same reading we find emphasis that herein we may see "the love the Father hath shown to the children of men [a phrase frequent in the readings!], through the very gift of Him, thy Brother, the Christ." We are told that all "life indeed is an external expression of the love of the Father" coming into expression "through the individuality of each and every soul." This high view of the origin of all life, and in particular of human life, is coupled with frank acknowledgment of our present weaknesses in material manifestation. Yet "we find the strength in the Lord" to the end that we may be transformed and experience "the glories [of] His bounteous purpose with each soul, that purpose that ye might be the companions, one with Him."

This relational goal, or purpose of our existence, as companions and cocreators with our Maker, as workers in harmony with the Whole, is also described in the following biblical language, "For we be joint heirs, as one with Him [the Christ], not strangers, not aliens, but joint heirs with the Christ to the kingdom of the Father, that is, that was—that ever shall be—even before the foundations of the earth were laid" (no. 1504–1; compare Rom. 8:17; Matt. 25:34).

The understanding that the final purpose of God the Father is that all souls may be reunited with him in ongoing, creative companionship—thus each soul may retain its own individuality in the relationship—is a central theme of the Edgar Cayce readings. The goal of each entity is "to become one with, yet aware of its *own* identity *in*, the Creative Force" (no. 261–15; see also no. 1456–1). For this reason we find in the readings also an alternation between the use of the word atonement, in the sense of vicarious atonement—the work of God through the Christ to the end of the restoration of personal relationships, a work that in a fundamental sense must be done for us—and the word at-onement, in the sense of spiritual unity, a reality of relationship for which our conscious cooperation is necessary. Both dimensions are seen as operative within the framework of divine or cosmic law. We see thus that "the activity of Him that is free indeed" is in accord with "the law of love, of causation, of mercy, of justice, of all that makes for self becoming in at-onement relationship [evidently a process is envisaged], of filling the purposes for which one is called in materiality" (no. 5749–10). This perception of the life and work of Jesus as being in accord with universal law is described elsewhere: "Though He were in the world, He was not of the world, yet subject to the laws thereof, of materiality" (no. 1504–1; compare John 17:14–18).

In this context of understanding the meaning of atonement, or of at-onement, a further dimension of truth is offered us. This is spoken of as "the need of the Son to suffer the death on the cross, to offer Himself as a sacrifice." That is, "He offered it not alone for thyself [the person addressed in the reading], for the world, for souls of men, but for His *own* being!" (no. 877–29). The context of this reading makes it clear that the good, the essence, of salvation is relational, and the redemptive work of Jesus the Christ, seen also as the work of God the Father, constitutes a free gift in behalf of others, a work designed to restore relationships, first (in theological priority, not in temporal) with our Maker, then with each other and with the whole of creation. This work, while done *for* us—again, in theological priority—requires our cooperation to be truly effective; no interpersonal relationship is authentic without reciprocity!

Perhaps it is in connection with this principle that the Cayce readings take up what we have seen was a faith-understanding of early Jewish Christianity, that the work of Jesus the Christ served also to further his own relationship with the Father. Even though at this stage of his being and of the course of his earthly pilgrimages, Jesus had indeed become perfect—and therefore the sacrifice was perfect—yet the recapitulation as Jesus of Nazareth of the whole of his past completed or fulfilled every aspect of his relationship with God the Father (compare no. 5749–10; Heb. 5:8–9; 9:24–26).

The perfected relationship of Jēsus with the Father is thus intended to make possible the restoration of our relationship with the Father, not to displace it. "That [relationship of each soul with its Maker] may *not* be supplied by another" (no. 877–29). Each one of us is to know God and be personally related to him—primarily, although not exclusively—"within." "For thy body is indeed the temple of the living God. There He has promised to meet thee. There He has promised to make Himself known to thee—His will, His purpose with thee" (no. 877–29; compare 1 Cor. 3:16; 6:15, 19; 2 Cor. 6:16). We read further that "the will of the Father [is] that no soul should perish but that there may be the burning of the dross, that it may be sifted as wheat, that it may be purified even as He through suffering in the material things that *are* for the soul's edification" (no. 262–77; compare 2 Pet. 3:9; 1 Cor. 3:10–17; Luke 22:31–32; Tit. 2:14).

HOLY WOMEN

As we continue consideration of the perceptions of the passion of Jesus found in the Edgar Cayce readings, we come to the role of the "holy women," a term that was used as such, we are told, only after the resurrection of Jesus. These are the women who contributed of both their means and services to the public ministry of Jesus and of his disciples (compare Mark 15:40–41; Luke 8:1–3; Matt. 27:55–56). They were the ones who brought spices to anoint Jesus' body for burial and served the disciples so well in the days of persecution following his death (no. 5122–1; no. 2794–3; compare Mark 16:1 and parallels). And on that "day when the sun was darkened and not by an eclipse alone, and when the earth shook and the temple veil was rent" (no. 333–2; compare Matt. 27:45–54 and parallels), a number of the women "stood beneath the cross . . . [of] the teacher, the lowly one, yet the GREAT I AM" (no. 1463–2; see also no. 3006–1; compare Mark 15: 40–41 and parallels).

In another reading the question was specifically asked, "Who were the women at the cross?" The answer given was, "Many were there. Those of His own household, Mary Magdalene, the mother of James and John, and those who were of that whole group were among the women at the cross" (no. 5749–10).

This day, "when the earth was darkened and the foundations of the deep were broken up, for the Son of man, the Son of God, was suspended between earth and the sky" (no. 518–1), came also to have special meaning for some of the Roman soldiers present. There were those "of the Roman guard who were struck by the sincerity of the *man* and of the followers of the man, as man" (no. 2365–2; compare Mark 15:39). Several references are made in the readings to these soldiers—they "*saw* the Prince of Peace die on the cross" (no. 333–2; compare John 19:32–33)—and to members of their household who later gave direct or indirect aid to the early Christian movement in Rome and elsewhere.

Some personally aided in the spreading of the teaching.

The name of one of the soldiers who "stood by the cross when the Son of man was put thereon" (no. 405–1) is cited as Marcellus. Marcellus's wife is said to have been later "in that position as being able to give help both to those persecuted and strength to those whom duty demanded oft to act in the capacity of the persecutors" (no. 405–1). The reading does not go on to resolve the theological or the practical and ethical dilemma involved in the woman's conduct or that of the others, except to imply that what she did for both sides was right.

Scattered throughout the Cayce readings are many statements that illumine the meaning of the cross of "Him that gave Himself as the ransom in the earth, despised of men yet without fault, showing forth His love" (no. 518–1; compare Mark 10:45; Heb. 4:15), "Him that blessed and cursed not, that gave to those though they bruised His body, though they sought to do away with those principles" (no. 1058–1; compare Luke 6:28; Rom. 12:14). In another reading we find what is, even if not a so-called "word from the cross," one expression of Jesus' intended communication "to those gathered at the cross, 'Peace I give, not as men count peace'— but the purpose in the heart is sure in the Lord—'I have shown thee the way' " (no. 649–1; compare John 14:5–6, 27).

In another reading we find a statement singularly indicative of Jesus' thoughts at this most critical of times:

> Then as He hung upon the cross, He called to those that He loved and remembered not only their spiritual purposes but their material lives. For He indeed in suffering the death on the cross became the whole, the entire way—*the* way, *the* life, *the* understanding—that we who believe on Him may, too, have the everlasting life. For He committed unto those of His brethren not only the care of the spiritual life of the world but the

material life of those that were of His own flesh, His own blood. (no. 5749–6; compare John 19:26–27)

A concrete example of this concern of Jesus for the material welfare of those nearest him is expressed in a reading addressed to the woman who is said to have been Jesus' sister Ruth in a former life: "He looked upon thy mother and thy friends and gave, 'Behold the woman,' and to thy cousin and to thy friend gave, 'To you she is given. Be to her a son in my stead' " (no. 1158–5; compare John 19:26–27). These words also suggest that John the apostle, the son of Zebedee and brother of James, was cousin to Ruth and therefore to Jesus.

Concern for both fact and details of human material as well as spiritual needs is typical of the Cayce readings' perception of the person and work of Jesus. We should, however, take particular note of the phrase "the care of the spiritual life of the world" as one indication of the nature of the ongoing mission of "those of His brethren."

The mission of Jesus' followers, his brethren, is described in another reading. "He hath entrusted to thee—to those that love Him—the redemption of the world, to make known His willingness, His care, His promises that may be the activity of each and every soul" (no. 5749–13). We note also that "rededication of self" is an appropriate characteristic for "being a true messenger of His in and among men" (no. 5749–6; compare Rom. 12:1–2). Elsewhere we read in the strongest terms of the spirit of dedication and self-sacrifice properly belonging to those who love the Lord Christ and would serve in his universal mission.

Those that honor, those that love Him even as He loved the world [compare John 3:16; 17:23], would give, do give their own heart's blood that the world may know that He *lives* and is at the right hand of the Father [compare Mark 12:36; 14:62; 16:19 and parallels], that ye—yea, thy brethren, thy friends, thy enemies—may have an advocate before that throne of mercy, pleading the cause of the wayward, hearing the cry of those persecuted [compare 1 John 2:1–2], and saying, "Be patient, be patient, my child, for in patience know ye thine own soul [compare Luke 21:19] and become aware that I am able to sustain thee, even though ye walk through the valleys and in the shadows of death" [compare Ps. 23:4]. For death hath no sting, it hath no power over those that know the resurrection [compare 1 Cor. 15:55–57]. (no. 1158–5)

In another reading we find an admonition that gives further insight into Jesus' mind and thought as he hung upon the cross. "Let that mind ever be in thee as was in Him as He offered Himself up, 'Father, forgive them—they know not what they do. Father, it is finished—I come to Thee. Give Thou Thy servant that glory which Thou hast promised' " (no. 5749–13; compare Luke 23:34; John 17:5; 19:30).

Something of the meaning of the entire event of Jesus' passion, indeed of his whole life, is given in the following excerpt.

For indeed He is the Creator, He indeed is the Maker of all that doth appear [compare John 1:3, 10; Col. 1: 15–16]. For all power in heaven and earth has been given unto His keeping through the faith He kept with His fellow man [compare Matt. 11:27; 28:18; John 3: 35; 13:3], by His doing good in all ways, at all times, under every circumstance [compare Acts 10:38; Mark 10:18]. Yet not railing—on any—though they demanded His life in the material, though they cuffed and buffeted Him, though they swore and spit upon Him, though they crowned Him with thorns, though they abused Him in every manner, yet opened He not His mouth, though He were their Lord, their Master. (no. 1499–1; compare Mark 15:1–39 and parallels; Isa. 53: 1–12; Acts 8:26–40)

The centrality of the meaning of the cross of Jesus in its cosmic as well as individual or personal sense is also indicated in the following advice. "*Do not* attempt to shed or to surpass or go around the cross. *This* is that upon which each and every soul *must* look and know it is to be borne in self *with* Him" (no. 5749-14). Here again the Cayce readings emphasize that the person and work of Jesus the Christ have an objective, vicarious efficacy for others *and* at the same time constitute the true and right pattern for the life of every human being, a pattern, however, that is to be copied (followed) not in isolation nor in a self-help manner, but "*with* Him" (compare Mark 8:34–35 and parallels, Rom. 8:17; Col. 1:24; Heb. 5:8–9; 1 Pet. 2:20–21).

As has already been intimated, the central meaning of the cross of Jesus the Christ in the Cayce readings is seen primarily not in the heroic nature of the physical suffering, although this dimension is of course not to be disregarded. The readings, rather, lay emphasis upon Jesus' making His will one with the Father, upon the perfection of His obedience, in spite of all that the power of evil was able to do—physically, mentally, or spiritually. Thus we read,

> Jesus became the ensample of the flesh, manifest in the world, and the will one with the Father, He became the first to manifest same in the material world. Thus, from man's viewpoint, becoming the only, the first, the begotten of the Father, and the ensample to the world, whether Jew, Gentile or of any other religious forces. In this we find the true advocate with the Father, in that He, as man, manifested in the flesh the ability of flesh to make fleshly desires one with the will of the spirit. For God is spirit, and they who worship Him must worship in spirit and truth. (no. 900–17; compare Phil. 2:5–11; Rom. 8:29; Col. 1:15–20; John 4:23–24)

This same reading goes on to make more explicit the relationship of Jesus the Christ with the other religious traditions of world history. That is, it affirms their positive religious significance in the larger economy of God in the world, even their progressive development in the direction of serving unto the fulfillment of God's final purposes with his creation, and at the same time [the person who requested this reading was Jewish] insists upon the uniqueness and specific supremacy of the person and role of Jesus. "As we see in all the religions of the world, we find all approaching those conditions where man may become as the law in his connection with the Divine, the Supreme, the Oneness, of the world's manifestation. In Jesus we find the answer" (no. 900–17).

The meaning of the above language is not entirely clear, but clarity is not lacking with regard to its focus upon Jesus of Nazareth as the resolution of all human questions. Elsewhere we read, "*Jesus*, the *man*, WAS the Son, *was* the Savior, *is* the manifestation of the God Consciousness in materiality!" (no. 1527–1).

This last reading goes on to say, "Yet it must needs be that *He*, too, suffer through the trials of being buffeted, being tried—by those who under the *law* [of man] were in authority but who under the spiritual law were His inferiors, His subjects—and die even the death on the cross" (no. 1527–1). Perhaps we may gain here a hint as to the meaning of the previous quotation from no. 900–17. One aspect of our destiny as human beings may be to change our fixation upon human law and custom to the freedom of cooperation with the divine law.

ENDING UNTO BEGINNING

The Cayce readings emphasize, as we have seen, that it was the so-called holy women who brought spices and other materials (ointments and aromatics) to anoint the body of Jesus after his death, according to the custom of the time and place. There is also mention of a woman who "was not able to bring spices because of the value, so brought flowers of the field which were just as acceptable as was the widow's mite, she of whom the Lord said, 'She hath given more than them all' " (no. 5122–1; compare Luke 21:1–4). The Gospels of Mark and Luke state that the women brought the spices. In John, Nicodemus is said to have brought the materials, a large quantity of myrrh and aloes (Mark 16:1; Luke 23:55–56; Matt. 27:55–61; John 19:38–42).

The statement is also made that the preparation of Jesus' body was made "hurriedly, as it were, for the day was at an end when it [Jesus' body] was delivered to Joseph of Arimathea and those that took care of same" (no. 897–1; compare John 19:38–42). The readings follow the Johannine tradition in stating that Nicodemus was also among those who "cared for the body when the burial time came" (no. 1402–1). In this very context the comment is added, "Know that Nicodemus *was* right; He [Jesus] had, He *has*, He *is* the words of life. He is the Word that maketh all things anew" (no. 1402–1; compare John 3:1–15; Rev. 21:5). Mention is also made of "the preparations of the linens about the head of the Master when entombed by Josephus and the friends" (no. 1801–1; compare John 19:38).

In one of the readings that refer to the activities of this time we find a passage of moving power that speaks of Jesus as representative of the "Law of One." This expression is frequently used in the Cayce readings to denote the basically unitive principle of being said to be characteristic of the Godhead. This is the principle within which trinitarian dimensions are included.

He the man represented in that taught was the Law of One, that each soul is a portion—its own portion of that Creative Force that we may make manifest by the manner in which we minister to those whom we contact in every way, in every manner, whether they be those in high estate or those that are struggling along the road of fear and doubt, or those that have fallen by the wayside. For each soul is precious in His sight, and He hath not willed that any should perish but that all—through that *will* as was manifested in the man that the entity . . . saw hung upon the tree upon the hill might have eternal life in Him. (no. 897–1; compare Acts 17: 28–29; Matt. 10:31; 12:12; Luke 12:7; 1 Tim. 2:3–4; 4:10; 2 Pet. 3:9)

Another reading sums up the basic issue and consequent choice with regard to the person and work of Jesus of Nazareth as they were perceived by many of his contemporaries, an issue and choice that confront people of every time and place. There were "questionings as to whether that proclaimed by the fisherfolk, or that proclaimed by those in power or in authority, was to become the rule of the peoples." These were the "two influences, two forces" between which many were set and by which they felt drawn—between which also they had to choose, as do we (no. 1402–1). This same reading contains the observation that "He without an ideal is sorry indeed; he with an ideal and lacking courage to live it is sorrier still."

This, then, is the end of the story of this extraordinary human life in its manifestation in flesh and blood upon the plane of human history. The whole of the New Testament, however, is one in its triumphant insistence that the story is continued in other forms. Both the gospels and the other apostolic writings are unanimous in their witness that Jesus rose from the dead in discernible ways and that after forty days he ascended into heaven. To the disciples' eyes of faith this ascension of their Lord meant not a departure from their experience but a wider, indeed a universal availability of his presence and power. The Edgar Cayce readings follow in the mainstream of this tradition of faith with their own special insights and modes of interpretation. Let us now consider them.

13

THE RESURRECTION AND THE ASCENSION

THE EDGAR CAYCE readings are indeed rich in materials and references to the resurrection of Jesus. They also include insights that are helpful in clarifying issues over which there has long been dispute.

About the fact of Jesus' resurrection, however—as a fact with both historical and transhistorical dimensions—there is no doubt or question. "The period of resurrection—here we find that in which ye *all* may glory. For without the fact of His overcoming death, the whole of the experience would have been as naught" (no. 5749–10). Like the New Testament Letter to the Hebrews, the readings portray Jesus the Christ, even though he was "the Maker of the earth, the Giver of life" (no. 518–1; compare John 1:1–5; 5:26; 11:25; 14:6), as "the man Jesus—who became the Christ through the things which He suffered, and through demonstrating in the earth the abilities to overcome *death*, the law of death" (no. 1877–2; compare Heb. 1:1–2; 2:10, 18).

Then, though He were the first of man, the first of the sons of God in spirit, in flesh, it became necessary that He fulfill *all* those associations, those connections that were to wipe away in the experience of man that which separates him from his Maker [compare Col. 1:15; Rom. 8:29].

> . . . Yea, as He gave His physical blood that doubt and fear might be banished, so He overcame death— not only in the physical body but in the *spirit* body— that it may become as *one* with Him [God the Father], even as on that resurrection morn, that ye call thy Eastertide. (no. 5749–6)

This perception of the need—and of the fact—to overcome death in the dimension of spirit as well as of the physical is in harmony with the Cayce readings' anthropology, the tripartite view of the nature of humanity as body, mind, and soul (or spirit). (The apostle Paul, differently from the bipartite (body and soul, *corpus et anima*) anthropology of much western European tradition, also seems to teach a tripartite view of the nature of humanity. See Rom. 1:9; 7:6 [in the Greek]; 1 Cor. 2:11; 5:3–5; Rom. 2:9; Thess. 5:23). It is also in keeping with the strong emphasis of the Christian church in its early centuries upon the concept of the descent of the risen Christ to Hades, which is also a perception of a mighty work done in spiritual realms (compare 1 Pet. 3:18–22). (The presence of this item of faith in the Apostles Creed is of course also highly significant as an indication of its importance to early Christians. Its early presence in the creed seems undeniable.)

The readings add that some aspects of this experience of Jesus after physical death are akin to what every human being must experience. "Each soul comes to stand as He before that throne of his Maker, with the deeds that have been done in the body, in the mind, presenting the body-spiritual before that throne of mercy, before that throne of the Maker, the Creator, the God" (no. 5749–6; compare Rom. 14:12; Heb. 13:17; 1 Pet. 4:5).

We find in the Cayce readings several intimations of the nature of the event or process involved in the resurrection of Jesus. "The passing of the material life into the spiritual life brought the *glorified* body, thus enabling the *perfect* body to be materialized in material life—a glorified body made perfect" (no. 5749–10). This statement at once reminds us of the language of the apostle Paul in his First Letter to the Corinthians (1 Cor. 15:35–57). The new condition of Jesus as a result of passing from the dimension of material life to that of spiritual life involved a new kind of body, perfect in its kind, called glorified. This was a condition of being, however, of such flexibility as to be able to rematerialize in material life at will and yet not be confined therein. As we shall see from further quotations, absence of confinement, lack of the restrictions and limitations of ordinary material life, of time and space, is one of the chief characteristics of this glorified spiritual body.

On the one hand, the Cayce readings use traditional language such as the following. "It is that . . . breaking forth from the sleep that it may rise as He with healing in its very life, to bring all phases of man's experience to His consciousness—that indeed became then the fulfilling of the law" (no. 5749–6). Here we find emphasis upon Jesus' resurrection as the climax of his fulfillment of divine law—as of the historic law of Israel. Its quality and effect for others, however, are to bring "healing in its very life," as they are to bring Jesus' now transcendent awareness to full knowledge of the totality of human experience, to the end that he may be the Father's instrument to help us all.

On the other hand, there are attempts to describe the phenomenon in more technical language. In answer to a question asking whether the mystery of the resurrection involved "transmutation of human flesh to flesh divine," the sleeping Cayce denied that this was so. "Not transmutation of flesh but creation."

There is no mystery to the transmutation of the body of the Christ. For having attained in the physical consciousness the at-onement with the Father-Mother-God, the completeness was such that with the disintegration of the body—as indicated in the manner in which the shroud, the robe, the napkin lay—there was then the taking of the body-physical form. This was the manner. It was not a transmutation, as of changing from one to another [compare John 20:6–7].

Just as indicated in the manner in which the body-physical entered the upper room with the doors closed, not by being a part of the wood through which the body passed but by forming from the ether waves that were within the room, because of a meeting prepared by faith. For as had been given, "Tarry ye in Jerusalem—in the upper chamber—until *ye* be endued with power from on high." (no. 2533–8; compare Luke 24: 49)

This language seems to say that as a consequence of Jesus' attainment of full and unbroken unity of consciousness with the "Father-Mother-God," his physical body disintegrated and a new spiritual body, an instrument more appropriate to his now universal consciousness, was created for him. The reading also seems to say that Jesus' materialization within the room was made more easily possible by the presence there of "ether waves" issuing from a gathering of his disciples in the spirit of faith and prayer (compare Luke 24:33–49).

Another reading, however, uses the word "revivify" with reference to Jesus' dead physical body, as if we are to understand that the essence of the event was to give new life, new light to the body, resulting in a renewed instrument of the self.

When the Prince of Peace came into the earth for the completing of His *own* development in the earth [compare Heb. 5:8–9], *He* overcame the flesh *and* temptation. So He became the first of those that overcame death in the body, enabling Him to so illuminate, to so revivify that body as to take it up again, even when those fluids of the body had been drained away by the nail holes in His hands and by the spear piercing His side. (no. 1152–1)

If we continue on with the reading quoted just previously to the above, we find use of the word "transformation" as the term preferred to "transmutation." It is not clear just how these words are to be distinguished as words, but there can be little doubt as to the meaning of the discourse as a whole. This is that the event of Jesus' resurrection involved the creative action of God the Father, giving new life and light, to the end that the body of Jesus was transformed into a spiritual body with qualities distinctly transcending the known physical. The same reading also suggests that a certain process was involved, including even temporal dimensions, as we find implied also in the Gospel of John.

> As indicated in the spoken word to Mary in the garden, "Touch me not, for I have not yet ascended to my Father." The body (flesh) that formed that seen by the normal or carnal eye of Mary was such that it could not be handled until there had been the conscious union with the Sources of all power, of all force [compare John 20:17].
>
> But afterward—when there had been the first, second, third, fourth, and even the sixth meeting—He *then* said, "Put forth thy hand and touch the nail prints in my hands, in my feet. Thrust thy hand into my side and *believe*." This indicated the transformation. (no. 2533–8; compare John 20:27)

The same reading develops this theme further:

> Just as it was with the Christ-body, "Children, have ye anything here to eat?" This indicated to the disciples and the apostles present that this was not transmutation but a regeneration, recreation of the atoms and cells of body that might, through desire, masticate

material things—fish and honey [in the honeycomb] were given [compare Luke 24:41–43; Acts 10:41].

As also indicated later, when He stood by the sea and the disciples and apostles who saw Him from the distance could not, in the early morning light, discern—but when He spoke, the voice made the impression upon the mind of the beloved disciple such that he spoke, "It is the Lord" [compare John 21:7]. The body had prepared fire upon the earth—fire, water, the elements that make for creation [compare Luke 12:49; Gen. 1:2]. For as the spirit is the beginning, water combined of elements is the mother of creation.

Not transmutation of flesh but creation, in the pattern indicated.

Further details of the resurrection event are given in the following passage.

Hence when those of His loved ones and those of His brethren came on that glad morning when the tidings had come to them, those that stood guard heard a fearful noise and saw a light, and—"the stone has been rolled away!" Then they entered into the garden, and there Mary first saw her *risen* Lord. Then came they of His brethren with the faithful women, those that loved His mother, those that were her companions in sorrow, those that were making preparations that the law might be kept, that even there might be no desecration of the ground about His tomb. They, too, of His friends, His loved ones, His brethren, saw the angels. [Note should be taken of the affectionate regard in which Jesus' mother Mary is said to have been held by the women who followed Jesus in his public ministry and served his needs and those of the twelve and of the other disciples (compare Mark 15:40–41; Luke 8: 1–3)].

How, why, took they [the angels] on form? That

there might be implanted into their [the disciples] hearts and souls that *fulfillment* of those promises. (no. 5749–6; compare Mark 16:9–11; John 20:11–18)

Reading 3615–1 speaks of one who "beheld those visions and knew of the quaking of the earth, knew of those that arose from the tomb" (no. 3615–1; compare Matt. 27:52–53).

In one of the readings a question was asked about a particular event in the first meeting of Jesus with his disciples in the upper room after his resurrection.

Q-4. Please explain, "He breathed on them, and saith unto them, 'Receive ye the Holy Ghost.' "

A-4. That change of doubt and fear which arose in the minds and hearts of those gathered in that room. For [their] fear of the interpreting of the phenomenon being experienced, He breathed. As the breath of life was breathed into the body of the man, see, so breathed He that of love and hope into the experience of those who were to become witnesses of Him in the material world. (no. 5749–10; compare John 20:19–23; Gen. 2:7)

Elsewhere we find a reference to one who "saw Him bless those about Him, after the resurrection" (no. 2620–2). This reading also, like the one immediately above, refers to the necessary spiritual equipping of those who were and are to serve in Jesus' ongoing mission and work in the world.

Another reading mentions one who "was with that group when there came the proclamation by Peter, John, and James that 'the Master goeth before thee into Galilee' " (no. 3615–1; compare Matt. 26:32; 28:7, 10, 16). This statement is in effect to affirm the understanding given us by the Gospel of Matthew of a post-resurrection meeting of Jesus with his disciples in Galilee (compare Luke 24:49; Acts 1:4, which passages seem to suggest that the disciples remained in Jerusalem. John 21:1–23 tells of a later post-resurrection meeting in Galilee). But the same reading goes on to describe the Lucan theme of the ascension of Jesus in speaking of one who "was among the five hundred who beheld Him as He entered into glory and saw the angels, heard their announcement of the event that must one day come to pass— and will only be to those who believe, who have faith, who look for and who expect to see Him as He is" (compare Luke 24:44–53; Acts 1:6–11; Mark 16:15–20; 1 Cor. 15:3–8).

This reading, we may note, also makes mention of the "second coming" of Jesus, a theme that we shall consider in more detail later. We should observe, however, at this point that the interpretation given in the reading tends to follow that found in the New Testament Lucan material (Luke 17:20–21; Acts 1:6–11) rather than that of the early letters of the apostle Paul (1 Thess. 4:16–17; 2 Thess. 1:7) or of the Book of Revelation (Rev. 1:7). That is, the latter passages seem to indicate a manifestation publicly visible to all human beings, as also is implied in some gospel verses (Matt. 24:30–31; possibly Mark 13:26). The Lucan passages suggest rather that Jesus' manifestation the second time will be "in the same way as you saw him go into heaven" (Acts 1:11), that is, perceptible only to those who believe and are open to accept the event.

The Cayce readings endeavor to explain in various ways both the larger, cosmic meaning of the resurrection of Jesus and also appropriate modes of present application of that meaning in our daily human lives. One recurrent theme of the readings is the personal worthiness of Jesus before God and humanity to experience resurrection. "When to man's estate alone upon the cross, yea into the grave, all hope seemed abandoned, yet even as the inn could not contain His birth, neither could the grave contain His body, because of IT *being purified*—in love, in service, in harmony with God's will (no. 1152–4; compare Acts 10:38). The Cayce readings, although often convoluted in style and difficult to understand, can also, as in this passage, rise to heights of beauty and power worthy of Shakespeare or Bunyan.

The theme of Jesus' personal worthiness is further expressed in the following reading.

> There should be the reminding that—though He bowed under the burden of the cross, though His blood was shed, though He entered into the tomb—through that power, that ability, that love, as manifested in Himself among His fellow man—He broke the bonds of death, proclaiming in that act *there is no death* when the individual, the soul, has and does put its trust in Him . . .
>
> Through that ability to make Himself one with the Father, He has gained that right, that honor to declare Himself unto as many as will hearken. (no. 5749–13; compare 1 Cor. 15:51–56; 1 Tim. 6:16; Heb. 1:9; 2 Pet. 1:17; Rev. 5:12–14)

Immediately following this passage we find these words of contemporary (March 12, 1941) significance, words of understanding, of compassion and of hope, directed to the person who requested the reading and to the others present.

> Thus in this hour of despair throughout the world, when those activities are such as to indicate hate, injustice, tyranny, desire to enslave or to impel others to submit to the dictates of this or that power—let all take heart and know that this, too, as the hour upon Calvary, must pass away, and that as upon the wings of the morning there comes that new hope, that new desire, to the hearts and minds of all who seek to know His face.

Then, in characteristic fashion, the sleeping Cayce turned in more direct fashion to address each person present, and wider circles as well, saying,

This must begin within thine own heart. Then, let all so examine their hearts and minds as to put away doubt and fear, putting away hate and malice, jealousy and those things that cause man to err. Replace these with the desire to help, with hope, with the willingness to divide self and self's surroundings with those who are less fortunate, putting on the whole armor of God—in righteousness. (compare Gal. 5:16–26; Eph. 6:10–20)

One of the themes most widely characteristic of the Edgar Cayce readings is their emphasis upon the need for personal as well as corporate appropriation and application of truth. Theology, theory, even faith, are never allowed to exist for their own sake, but must serve to the enhancement of the relational quality, both interior and exterior, of everyday human life. Thus, "The resurrection of Jesus the Christ is a significant fact to each individual only according to how he applies same, as it is significant to him, in his daily life, experience, and conversation with his fellow man" (no. 5749–12; compare Rom. 11:1–2).

In this context of faith-understanding, the readings give various admonitions and exhortations. Thus the question was put to the several persons present for reading 5749–12:

Then, in a material world—a world of hate, of divided opinions—what is the course that you each will pursue, in relationship to your fellow man?

Is it the course outlined by the tenets, the principles which He, the Teacher of teachers, gave as respecting the manner of life, of activity, that you each would give in your dealings and relationships with your fellow men?

This reference to "the course outlined by the tenets, the principles" taught by Jesus is an expression of the understanding consistent in the Cayce readings of Jesus' manner of teaching. That is, the emphasis of Jesus' teaching is seen as laid upon larger principles of conduct, such as the Golden Rule (Matt. 7:12; Luke 6:31) or Jesus' summation of the law and the prophets (Mark 12:28–34 and parallels). The application of these principles in concrete situations of daily life must be made by each individual as he or she, to the extent of his or her attunement with the Spirit of God, perceives the will of God and the specifics of his guidance.

Since, however, the Cayce readings do not proclaim any form of unbridled individualism, ethical decisions made by this means are seen as emerging properly in the context of participation in the fellowship of concerned others, especially of those of the "household of faith" (no. 518–1; compare Gal. 6:10; Eph. 2:19). Cayce himself combined such participation in the fellowship of the people of God with daily reading of at least three chapters of the Bible, a lifelong practice from the age of ten. Subsequent reference to the "tempo . . . way and manner" taught and manifested by Jesus (no. 5749–12) makes it clear that the process involved is one that lays stress upon spiritual sensitivity in the larger and deeper sense, rather than upon rational processes alone. The delicacy and artistry involved in this activity of discernment and application of basic principles of conduct are suggested by the following quotation: "Magnify, glorify Him in every word, every activity, in all thy dealings with thy fellow man. By thy very step, thy very look, by thy word, create *hope* in the hearts, minds and lives of others (no. 5749–13; compare 1 Cor. 13).

Reading no. 5749–12 (compare Luke 11:1–13 and parallels) continues:

> We know, and only need to be reminded, that the whole law is in Him. For as He gave that which is the basis, the principle, of the intent and desire and purpose which should prompt our activity, so we in the world— as we live, as we speak, as we pray—are to let it be in that tempo, in that way and manner which was

prompted by Him, as He taught His disciples how to pray.

Then, as we analyze this prayer in our experience, we see what the life, the death, the resurrection of Jesus the Christ—who is the Way, the Truth, the Light— must mean in this period in the experience of man.

The Cayce readings frequently affirm that meditation is an integral element of the wider ranges of prayer, that one must listen to God as well as speak to him (no. 262–127; no. 5265–1; no. 2051–5; no. 987–2; no. 282–4; no. 262–89). One reading gives the following version of what is called the Lord's Prayer:

Our Father who art in heaven, hallowed be Thy name. Thy kingdom come. Thy will be done—as in heaven, so in earth. Give us for tomorrow the needs of the body. Forget those trespasses as we forgive those that have trespassed and do trespass against us. Be thou the guide in the time of trouble, turmoil and temptation. Lead us in paths of righteousness for Thy name's sake. (no. 378–44).

This prayer was introduced with the words, "Let not the material things so blind thee that they become a stumbling block in thine experience. Give praise to thy Maker in the name of Him that taught thee to pray."

Further insight into the cosmic meaning of the resurrection of Jesus, together with aspects of its proper application in contemporary living, is given in the following: "Then, as ye meditate upon the meaning of the resurrection of this man of God, know that the way is open to thee to approach the throne of God—not as an excuse, not as a justification—but rather in love, in harmony, in that which brings hope for a sin-sick world" (no. 5749–12). The people present at the reading were reminded that this way of life means also "such a manner as to bring peace and harmony, even among those who *appear* to be at variance to the cause of the Christ in the material world.''

People close to Edgar Cayce, and cooperating in his work, were told in a reading given on April 5, 1936,

> Open thine eyes and behold the glory, even of thy Christ present here, now, in thy midst, even as He appeared to them on that day! . . .
>
> Ye, too, oft doubt; ye, too, oft fear. Yet He is surely with thee. And when ye at this glad season re-dedicate thy life, thy body, thy mind to His service, ye, too, may know, as they, that He *lives*—and is at the right hand of God to make intercession for *you*—if ye will believe, if ye will believe that He is, ye may experience.
>
> . . . [He is] thy Brother, thy Savior, thy Jesus, thy Christ, that would come and dwell in the hearts and lives of you all—if you will but let Him, if you will but invite Him, if you will but open thy own heart, each of you, that He may enter and abide with you . . .
>
> Crucify Him not in thy mind nor in thy bodily activities. Be not overcome by these things that are of the earth—earthy. Rather clothe thy body, thy mind, with the thoughts, the deeds, the privileges that His suffering as a man brought to thee. (no. 5749–6; compare Heb. 6:6; Phil. 2:1–11)

Elsewhere in the same reading this theme of the vicarious or substitutionary atonement of Jesus the Christ—the meaning for others of his suffering, death, and resurrection—is developed further by asking a very large question, and then immediately answering it.

> Why did He put on flesh and come into the earth in the form of man, but to be one with the Father, to show to man *his* (man's) [derivative] divinity, man's relationship to the Maker, to show man that indeed the

Father meant it when He said, "If ye call, I will hear. Even though ye be far away, even though ye be covered with sin, if ye be washed in the blood of the Lamb, ye may come back." (compare Isa. 1:18; 65: 24; Rev. 7:33; 11:11)

[We have already noted that in the Cayce readings the "divinity" of human beings is more a moral and spiritual issue than an ontological one, as in "Man as a *godly* man may be close to the divine." (no. 1301–1; compare John 10:34–36)]

Thus in every possible way the Cayce readings emphasize the present significance, effects, and reality of the resurrection of Jesus, of him who is the risen Lord and is present with those who will receive him. "I *am* the resurrection, the life" (no. 1747–3; compare John 11:25–26). (This same reading continues with a statement, spoken as the word of Jesus, referring back to an encounter during Jesus' public ministry, "I *told* thee to destroy the body and in three days I would raise it again" [no. 1747–3; compare John 2:19]. This word seems to be an instance of Jesus himself interpreting his own previous statement given in metaphorical language.) "To the heart and the soul He brought a light that faileth not, a water that is living, a home that is eternal, a bread that is *indeed* a staff of life! For HE IS that life—that LIFE" (no. 1152–4; compare John 1:4–5, 9; 3:19; 8:12; 4: 14; 6:35; 11:25; 14:6). He is "Life, Light and Immortality to the world today—ever. For He changeth not" (no. 1290–1; compare 2 Tim. 1:10; Jas. 1:17).

Another mode of present application of the reality of the resurrection of Jesus is given in the following:

For death hath no sting, it hath no power over those that know the resurrection [which] brought to the consciousness of man that power that God hath given to man, that may reconstruct, resuscitate, even every atom of a physically sick body, that may resurrect even every atom of a sin-sick soul, may resurrect the soul that it lives on and on in the glory of a resurrected, a regenerated Christ in the souls and hearts of men (no. 1158–5; compare 1 Cor. 15:55–57).

A very suggestive passage in the readings speaks of the experience of Jesus—and properly of us all as well—in terms of a kind of universal principle of reciprocity,

For it has ever been and is, even in materiality, a reciprocal world. "If ye will be my people, I will be thy God" [compare Ex. 6:7; Lev. 26:3–13; Jer. 7:23]. If ye would know *good*, do good. If ye would have life, give life. If ye would know Jesus the Christ, then be like Him, who died for a cause—without shame [on his own part], without fault—yet dying, and through that able to make what this season [the reading was given at Easter time, 1937] represents—*resurrection*!

Resurrection means what? It is reciprocal of that which has been expressed. How hath it been put again by him whom ye knew but disliked (for ye loved Peter the better)? [The Cayce readings, in their relatively extensive references to the period of the early church, especially that of its first or apostolic generation, are clear and specific in their recounting of contemporary criticisms of the person and lifestyle of the apostle Paul (no. 1151–10; no. 1541–11; compare Acts 15:1–29; Gal. 2:1–21).] "There is no life without death; there is no *renewal* without the dying of the old" [compare 2 Cor. 4:10–11; 6:9). Dying is not blotting out; it is transition. And ye may know transition by that as comes into the experience by those very activities, that "With what measure ye mete it shall be measured to thee again" [compare Matt. 7:2; Gal. 6:7]. That was His life, that is thy life, that is each one's life.

He put away self, letting it be nailed to the cross, that the *new*, the renewing, the fulfilling, the BEING the law, becomes the law! [compare Phil. 2:1–11; Rom. 10:4; 1 Cor. 9:21]

For it is the law to BE the law, and the law is love! Even as He showed in all of His manifestations, in the material experiences in the earth [compare John 13:34; Rom. 13:8].

Is it not a reciprocal world? What ye sow, ye reap. (no. 1158–9; compare Gal. 6:7)

We note a few references in the readings to the walk of two disciples to the neighboring village of Emmaus shortly after Jesus' death, when they met him on the way and recognized him in the breaking of bread in the house of one of them (no. 1158–2; compare Luke 24:13–35). Details, however, are not given. We read elsewhere that "there were about five thousand who saw and heard the words of the Master after the resurrection" (no. 1877–2). This statement evidently indicates a total number and may include the five hundred cited as the number who beheld the ascension of Jesus (no. 3615–1). The apostle Paul speaks of Jesus as having appeared, in one post-resurrection manifestation, "to more than five hundred brethren [masculine gender in the Greek] at one time" (1 Cor. 15:6).

The resurrection and the ascension of Jesus were clearly thought of by the New Testament writers as events experienced by human beings in one focus of time and place in human history. These same persons, and the communities of faith that they represented, were equally convinced that the events had ongoing effects of momentous significance and power in the subsequent course of human history. These efforts, they believed, derived not only from their original impulse but were, and are, continually renewed from what they experienced as "the abiding presence" of the Lord Jesus. Let us now consider what the Edgar Cayce readings say about this grand theme.

14

HIS ABIDING PRESENCE

A CENTRAL THEME of New Testament faith is the abiding presence of Jesus, as the risen Christ, with his followers. This presence, as we have seen, was experienced first through numerous post-resurrection appearances of Jesus. After his ascension, which is described most notably in the first chapter of the Acts of the Apostles, Jesus' presence comes especially to be associated with the coming of the Spirit of God, often cited in the New Testament as the Holy Spirit.

The most dramatic expression of the coming of the Holy Spirit upon Jesus' followers is that of the event on the feast of Pentecost, when there were evidently external manifestations such as a sound "like the rush of a mighty wind." There appeared also "tongues as of fire, distributed and resting on each one of them." The disciples are said to have been "all filled with the Holy Spirit and began to speak in other tongues, as the Spirit gave them utterance" (Acts 2:1–4).

What may have been an alternative, less dramatic, way of receiving the Holy Spirit is described in the Gospel of John, where Jesus communicates the Spirit during a post-resurrection appearance simply by breathing upon his disciples. Here we read, "Jesus said to them again, 'Peace be with you. As the Father has sent me, even so I send you.'

And when he had said this, he breathed on them and said to them, 'Receive the Holy Spirit' " (John 20:21–22; compare John 17:18; 4:35–38. This Spirit is also denoted as the Spirit of the Risen Christ (compare Rom. 8:2, 9; 1 Cor. 15:45; Gal. 4:6; Phil. 1:19; 1 Pet. 1:11), the Spirit who, as in the quotation from the First Letter of Peter (1:11), inspired the Old Testament prophets before his earthly manifestation in Jesus of Nazareth.

We have already seen that many of the Edgar Cayce readings cited in connection with other events in the life of Jesus have much to say also about his abiding presence in the life of humanity as the risen Christ, as of his work in the world before his manifestation in Palestine as Jesus. This is only to be expected in light of the strong concern of the readings for present appropriation and application of truth, as of the Spirit of God.

In connection with a quotation of the Great Commission of universal missionary purport, cited in the Gospel of Matthew as the climax of Jesus' post-resurrection appearances, we read, "Position or power or wealth or fame may be set at naught compared to the peace that came and *is* the understanding of those who have seen and known and become aware of His presence abiding, even as . . . promised, 'Lo, I am with you always, even unto the end of the world' " (no. 1602–4; compare Matt. 28:20). " 'I will abide with thee always!' Know that this means thy own self! For He hath not left thee comfortless, but the Spirit of truth abides ever with thee" (no. 1904–2; compare John 14:15–18). "To those of the earth hath He given the message, 'Lo, I am with thee always—*always*!' To *you*, to all who have named and do name His name is given that charge, 'Feed my sheep, care for my lambs' " (no. 1158–5; compare John 21:15–17). Here, in typical Cayce fashion, the promise of the Lord's abiding presence is conjoined with a statement of the human responsibilities that properly follow believing, accepting awareness of that presence. We note also from the phrase, "to those of the earth hath He given the message," that

Jesus' abiding presence may touch more persons and lives with its influences than is ordinarily understood by the term "Jesus' followers."

In the following reading we note a strong reminder that the abiding presence of the risen Christ is in no way to be divorced from the human Jesus. Jesus and the Christ are utterly one. Apparent defeat has been turned into victory. "Though He wept bodily over Jerusalem, though He sighed with the very blood of His body in Gethsemane, He smiled upon the cross—as He smiles upon thee and gives, 'I am with thee; be not afraid, it is I—even I who AM the Life, who *am* the Way, who *am* the word!' " (no. 1158–5; compare Mark 6:50 and parallels; John 1:1; 14:6). This affirmation of Jesus' smiling even while hanging upon the cross, surprising as it is at first sight, is, as we have seen, in keeping with other Cayce perceptions of the inner victory of Jesus even in the midst of physical and mental suffering during the last week of his life on earth.

With reference to the proper human response to the promises of the risen Lord's abiding presence, the Cayce readings give important specifics. This response is to be not only that of external obedience and activity, as when we are told, "They that would know Him [God the Father] must *believe* that He is, and most of all ACT that way!" (no. 1158–9; compare Heb. 11:6). The inner, personal, and relational dimensions of the response are equally, if not surpassingly, stressed.

> How personal is thy God? Just as personal as ye will let Him be! How close is the Christ as was manifested in the physical body Jesus? Just as near, just as dear as ye will let him be! . . .
>
> In the love of thine own children, is it those who ask or those who do not ask that make a response? Not that ye love one more than the other—not for impunity, but a reciprocal action! (no. 1158–9)

This quotation gives us insight into the Cayce readings' perception of the personal nature of God the Father. Such is not to say, as we have seen, that the personhood of God is limited like the personhood of human beings, or that there are not transpersonal aspects of God that may appear, from our human perspective, to be impersonal. It is to affirm, in the strongest way, that God is profoundly personal in his self-awareness and awareness of others—as his own creation—and in his desire for interpersonal relationships with his creation that issue in mutual love, companionship, and growing harmony in cooperative work. This reading also tells us that God desires our response in affectionate love—not that our faith and love are primarily intended to gain us exemption from punishment or harm (impunity, as the reading puts it); they are rather the way to the deepest and noblest of personal relationships. And the Cayce readings faithfully follow the teaching of Jesus that our love of God must also issue in the love of our "neighbor" (compare Mark 12:28–34 and parallels).

We read of the role and work of Jesus the Christ to bring into effect the kind of personal relationships above described. "He hath promised to stand in the places of those who are discouraged, disconsolate, who have lost a vision, lost hope" (no. 2156–1; compare Mark 10:45; 1 Cor. 15:3).

This is a reaffirmation of the historic theological theme of the redemptive work of Jesus the Christ, his role under God the Father—sent by and representative of the Father—for the liberation of others from the bondage of their selves and their past, unto restored and creative relationship with their Maker. The ongoing significance and effects—and reality in interpersonal relationships—of the work of Jesus the Christ is indicated in the following reading. "The lowly Nazarene was that fulfilling of that priesthood [the priesthood of Israel] in His offering of Himself as the lamb that was not to roll back but to take away the sins of the people. Not as an escape, but as an atonement in which each soul does find, would find, the Lamb standing *ever* as that offering in its relationships as an individual to its fellow man" (no. 1000–14; compare John 1:29, 36; 1 Pet. 1:18–21; Heb. 4:14–16; Rev. 7: 14; 12:11). "If the heart is open, He will come and abide with thee" (no. 1770–2). Not only was Jesus resurrected, "He *is* indeed the resurrection. He is indeed mindful of the sorrows as well as the joys of mankind" (no. 993–5; compare John 11:25–27; 1 Pet. 5:7).

The Cayce readings, however, make it clear that this redemptive work and the abiding presence of Jesus the Christ are not limited in their effects to historic Israel and the Christian church. We are here dealing with more universal realities. "For He indeed stands at the door of every consciousness of man that seeks to know—and will enter if man will but open" (no. 1842–1; compare Matt. 5:6; 6:33; 7:7–12). This is in order that "individuals become aware of the Christ Consciousness and become one with the operative forces of the Christ Spirit abroad in the earth" (no. 262–29). "Christ is the ruling force in the world . . . all power in heaven, in earth, is given to Him who overcame" (no. 5749–4; compare Matt. 11:27; 28:18; John 3:35; 13:3; 16:15; 17: 2).

This affirmation, however, of the present lordship of the risen Christ is seen in the Cayce readings as effective in relation to all people everywhere in real and structured potentiality, but actually and inwardly effective only for those who will let it be so. "He hath given His angels charge concerning those that seek to be a channel of blessing to their fellow man, that purge their hearts, their bodies, of every selfish motive and give the Christ—*crucified, glorified*—a place in its stead" (no. 696–3; compare Rom. 12:1–2; 1 Cor. 9:27: 2 Cor. 10:5). "He is of Himself in space, in the force that impels through faith, through belief, in the individual entity. As a spirit entity, hence not in a body in the earth . . . [He] may come at will to him who *wills* to be one with [Him] and acts in love to make same possible" (no. 5749–4). "In the spirit world He seeks to make manifest that sought by those who do His biddings" (no. 5749–4; compare John 14:

15, 21, 23; 15:10, 12–14). "Is He abroad today in the earth?
Yea, in those that cry unto Him from every corner" (no.
5749–5; compare Luke 18:7–8).

We may properly ask at this point what the Cayce readings
mean by the term Christ Consciousness. We read that "The
Christ Consciousness is a universal consciousness of the Father Spirit" (no. 5749–4). This term is to be distinguished
from the "Jesus Consciousness," which is the phrase used
to denote the appropriation and application of the Christ Consciousness in the physical body, in life on earth, seen as
perfect in Jesus in Nazareth, as yet imperfect in all others
(no. 5749–4). At the same time, however, we read that the
Christ consciousness is in every human being in structured
potentiality, in embryonic form. This is another way in which
the Cayce readings suggest concrete aspects of the concept
of the creation of human beings in the image of God. The
Christ Consciousness is described therefore as also "the
awareness within each soul, imprinted in pattern on the mind
and waiting to be awakened by the will, of the soul's oneness
with God" (no. 5749–14; compare Gen. 1:26–27; 5:1; Rom.
2:15).

Thus we read, "Not so much self-development but rather
developing the Christ Consciousness in self being selfless,
that He may have His way with thee, that He—the Christ—
may direct thy ways, that He will guide thee in the things
thou doest, thou sayest" (no. 281–20; compare Mark, 8:34–
35 and parallels). The expression of the Christ Consciousness
is elsewhere described as manifesting the fruits of the Spirit.
Such is to "practice, then, brotherly love, kindness, patience,
long-suffering, gentleness" (no. 3580–1; compare Gal. 5:22–
23). A further point of great significance for everyday living
is given in the following statement of the possible and proper
protective role of the Christ manifested as the surpasssing
influence of the Christ Consciousness at work in the world.
"No influence without or within may be of a detrimental
force to self—so long as self will surround self with the
thought and ability of the Christ Consciousness, and then

practice same in its dealings with its fellow man'' (no. 2081–2; compare 1 Cor. 10:12–13). Another reading, we should note, specifically identifies the Christ Consciousness with the Master Jesus (no. 3459–1).

If we ask how we may receive or participate in this Reality, how we may open ourselves aright, the answer given is, "Through searching, seeking, and humbling thyself before the throne of grace and mercy, as was manifested in Him; acknowledging Him as thy Lord, thy Master, yea, thy Elder Brother. He has given also, 'If ye open I will come and abide with thee' " (no. 2845–1; compare Rev. 3:20; John 14:18; 15:4). "He may be approached by those who in sincerity and earnestness seek to know Him—and to be guided by Him. As He has given, by faith all things are made possible through belief in His name" (no. 5749–4; compare Mark 10:27; John 14:13–14; 16:23; Matt. 21:22).

In several instances the readings give answers to specific questions of the kind that we have just posed. For example, the sleeping Cayce was asked, "How may I contact Him so that I see Him and hear Him speak?" The answer given is, "The making of the will of self one with His will makes a whole attunement with Him. He *will*, with the making of self in accord and desiring same, speak with thee, 'Be not afraid, it is I' " (no. 5749–4; compare Mark 6:50 and parallels). In another part of the same reading similar emphasis is placed upon faith, desire, and sincere effort to harmonize one's will and purposes with those of God the Father—all with focus upon Jesus the Christ as the supreme channel to the Father. "Making the will, the desire of the heart, one with His, believing in faith, in patience, all becomes possible in Him—through Him to the Father, for He gave it as it is" (no. 5749–4; compare Matt. 21–22).

In striking, even poetic, language we find elsewhere the same theme repeated and stressed. "He comes again in the hearts and souls and minds of those that seek to know His ways . . . those that call on Him will not go empty-handed . . . Yet *here* ye may hear the golden scepter ring—ring—in the hearts of those that seek His face" (no. 5749–5; compare 1 Chron. 16:11; Ps. 105:4; Rom. 10:12–13). Here, as elsewhere in the Cayce readings, the abiding presence of the risen Christ experienced in believing faith is treated as one mode of his "coming again." "Thy Brother, thy Savior, thy Jesus, thy Christ . . . would come and dwell in the hearts and lives of you all—if you will but let Him, if you will but invite Him, if you will but open thy own heart, each of you, that He may enter and abide with you" (no. 5749–6; compare Rev. 3:20).

Another reading expresses this theme succinctly:

> Invite Him, by name, by purpose, by desire, to be thy companion in all that ye do, all that ye say. He rejecteth not those who willingly, honestly, sincerely, invite Him to be with them. As He never rejected an invitation by any as He walked in the earth as an individual, neither does He reject the invitation of a soul that seeks—in sincerity—His companionship." (no. 622–6; compare John 6:37; Matt. 11:28–30)

As we have seen, the Cayce readings affirm that the primary purpose of the divine creation of the souls that we know on earth as human beings was that we may be companions with our Maker. This is of course to express with a synonym the wish of Jesus cited in the Gospel of John that he prefers to call his disciples "friends" (John 15:14–15). This is also the theme of one of the most profound streams in the history of Christian spirituality, seen, for instance, in the pre-Reformation movement in the Rhine valley known as the Friends of God. The proper name, we may recall, of that wonderful movement initiated in the seventeenth century in England by George Fox and popularly called the Quakers is the Society of Friends.

Another reading expresses the same theme in the following fashion: "Let the theme of the mental body ever be *Jesus*, the Savior, the merciful companion to those who seek to know God's way with men. For He *is* that friend that would ever guide, direct and *accompany* thee in trials, temptations, in thy joys as well as sorrows'' (no. 1173–10; compare John 14:18, 21, 26; 17: 12).

15

THE SECOND COMING

THE CAYCE READINGS forthrightly affirm the second coming of Jesus the Christ. "How hath the angel given? 'As ye have seen Him go, so will ye see Him come.' Were those just words? No!" (no. 1158–9; compare Acts. 1:1–11).

The mode of this return is here suggested to be similar to that of Jesus' ascension, as described in the biblical Acts of the Apostles. We find a further explanation of this understanding with the statement that it "will be only to those . . . who look for and expect to see Him as He is" (no. 3615–1; compare Matt. 24:29–31; Mark 13:26; 1 Thess. 4:16–17). This language seems to imply a mode of manifestation that is not necessarily public or perceptible to all persons on earth at the time. Rudolf Steiner affirmed through his own clairvoyant activity an understanding of the return of Christ Jesus similar to that found in the Edgar Cayce readings. According to Johannes Hemleben's *Rudolf Steiner*, in 1923 Steiner stated, "Christ will return, but in a form that transcends physical reality, a form that only he can look upon who has come to understand spiritual life."

Yet the manifestation is not, we are told by Cayce, to be understood as merely a vague influence. "He shall come as ye have seen Him go, in the *body* He occupied in Galilee. The body that He formed, that was crucified on the cross, that rose from the tomb, that walked by the sea, that appeared to Simon, that appeared to Philip, that appeared to 'I, even John' " (no. 5749–4; compare John 21:1–25; 1 Cor. 15:3–8). This language clearly seems to imply a manifestation of Jesus that will be recognizable to those who know him in some fashion. (The first-person reference to the apostle John in this quotation is one of the few instances in the readings in which the "source" is willing to reveal its identity. Other sources so identified are the archangel Michael [no. 254–42, 66; no. 294–100; 262–27, 28, 29, 33], the angel Halaliel [no. 4976–15; no. 262–56] and possibly Jesus himself [no. 993–3; no. 137–125]. It should be recognized, however, that this kind of phenomenon is rare in the whole corpus of 14,256 recorded Cayce readings. That which is ordinarily called "mediumship" is almost totally nonexistent. A possible exception is reading no. 5756–5, and this experience was not intended or requested by Cayce.)

In several readings it is stated that "the day of the Lord is indeed at hand" (no. 2156–1). This statement is explained in the following question and answer given in another reading.

Q-3. What is meant by "the day of the Lord is near at hand?"

A-3. That as has been promised through the prophets and the sages of old, the time—and half time [compare Dan. 7:25]—has been and is being fulfilled in this day and generation [date of the reading, July 9, 1933], and that soon there will again appear in the earth that one through whom many will be called to meet those that are preparing the way for His day in the earth. The Lord, then, will come, "even as ye have seen Him go" [compare Acts 1:11].

Q-4. How soon?

A-4. When those that are His have made the way clear, passable, for Him to come. (no. 262–49)

The reference in the reading here quoted to "that one" apparently means the same person described elsewhere as the "one who is to be a forerunner of that influence in the earth known as the Christ Consciousness, the coming of that force or power into the earth that has been spoken of through the ages" (no. 5749–5). (The phrase "that influence in the earth known as the Christ Consciousness" is probably similar to that frequently identified by Rudolf Steiner as "the Christ Impulse.") The name of this "forerunner" is not given in the readings. The same reading, however, goes on to use more conventional language concerning the second coming of the Christ, speaking of "those days when He will come in the flesh, in the earth, to call His own by name." This language, to be sure, implies some kind of bodily manifestation. Another reading speaks of the return of the Lord as follows. "*Then* shall the Christ Spirit be manifest in the world" (no. 262–29).

To return to the issue of the time of the event, "The time no one knows. Even as He gave, not even the Son Himself, *only* the Father. Not until His enemies—and the earth—are wholly in subjection to His will, His powers" (no. 5749–2; compare Matt. 24:36; Acts 1:6–7; 1 Cor. 15:20–28). But then in answer to the further question, "Are we entering the period of preparation for His coming?" the same reading says, "Entering the test period rather." (The date of this reading, June 28, 1932, is the occasion of the first Annual Congress of the Association for Research and Enlightenment.) Another reading, given in the context of consideration of possible changes in the earth's surface structure predicted for the second half of the twentieth century, states, "These will begin in those periods in '58 to '98, when these will be proclaimed as the periods when His light will be seen again in the clouds" (no. 3976–15; compare Mark 13:26 and parallels). Here we note reference apparently to an event visible, at least to some, and of grand scope.

We note with regard to the time of the second coming several comments in one of the 262 series of readings that speak of many persons feeling that the Father has delayed the return of the Christ—out of "the merciful kindness of the Father." In this context the further word is given that also speaks movingly of the high importance of human responsibilities and contributions to the event, especially the mission of Jesus' followers.

> Yet, as He has given, in patience, in listening, in being still, may ye know that the Lord doeth all things well. Be not weary that He apparently prolongs His time, for, as the Master has given, "As to the day, no man knoweth, not even the Son, but the Father, and they to whom the Father may reveal the Son, prepareth the way that all men may know the love of the Father" (compare Matt. 24:36; 11:27; John 14:1–3). And as ye would be the channel to hasten that glorious day of the coming of the Lord, then do with a might that thy hands find to do to make for the greater manifestations of the love of the Father in the earth. For, into thy keeping, and to His children and to His sons, has He committed the keeping of the saving of the world, of the souls of men. . . . So as He gave, "I leave thee, but I will come again and receive as many as ye have quickened through the manifesting in thy life the will of the Father in the earth." Hence know that as thine mind, thine activities, long more and more for the glorifying of the Son in the earth, for the coming of the day of the Lord, He draws very nigh unto thee. (no. 262–58, given on February 11, 1934)

Here, as frequently elsewhere in the Cayce readings, the mission of the followers of the risen Christ is seen as intimately, inextricably associated with his followers' manifestation of the will of the Father in their own lives, in their thoughts and feelings as in their activities.

We find also in one of the Cayce readings what we may call, using historic Christian terminology, a kind of mille-

narian view. This faith holds that the return of Christ Jesus
upon this earth in visible form will result in a glorious reign
of a thousand years. At the end of this period the forces of
evil will be unleashed, and a battle of cosmic scope between
the forces of good and evil will ensue. God the Father and
his Christ will have total victory over all opposing will, and
complete harmony and happiness will be the experience of
all who are on God's side (compare Rev. 20:1–22:21).

The question was asked, "When Jesus the Christ comes
the second time, will He set up His kingdom on earth and
will it be an everlasting kingdom?" The sleeping Cayce answered, "Read his promises in that ye have written of His
words, even as I gave. He shall rule for a thousand years"
(no. 5749–4; compare Rev. 20:7–10). This is one of the few
cases in the Cayce readings in which the speaker is revealed
to be other than Cayce's own subconscious self. Here the
speaker would seem to be the John who was the author of
the New Testament book, the Revelation to John. With regard, however, to the larger issue of millennial phenomena,
no further information is given. The reading in this case is
the only one to offer this position of faith, and it is proper
to add that with regard to particularities of time, millennial
views have played only a minority role in the history of
Christian faith. It is proper to note in the reading just cited
that the word "promises" is used rather than "predictions."
This usage is common in the Cayce readings, wherein the
teaching of Jesus, as of Scripture as a whole, is frequently
spoken of as replete with positive divine promises for the
salvation, the welfare of humanity.

The general posture of the Cayce readings is to combine
helpful anticipation of the future with positive emphasis upon
present possibilities within this world and the next. Thus we
read,

> If ye will believe that He is, ye may experience. For
> as many as have named the name, and that do unto
> their brethren the deeds that bring to them, to you

[also], that closeness, oneness of purpose with Him, may know—ye, too—in body, in mind, that where He is, there ye may be also. . . .

For thy Christ, thy Lord, thy Jesus is nigh unto thee—just now! (no. 5749-6; compare Heb. 11:6; Matt. 25:31–46; John 14:3)

This dual emphasis is revealed in yet another reading, a reading that also speaks of the coming again of the Lord Jesus as possible in a variety of ways, both external and internal.

Then again He may come in body to claim His own. Is He abroad today in the earth? Yea, in those that cry unto Him from every corner. For He, the Father, hath not suffered His soul to see corruption, neither hath it taken hold on those things that make the soul afraid. For, He *is* the Son of Light, of God, and is holy before Him. And He comes again in the hearts and souls and minds of those that seek to know His ways.

These be hard to be understood by those in the flesh, where prejudice, avarice, vice of all natures holds sway in the flesh. Yet those that call on Him will not go empty-handed! (no. 5749-5; compare Acts 2:27, 31, and the like; Gal. 5:19–21; Rom. 10:12–13)

Part IV

THE LARGER MEANING OF THE LIFE AND WORK OF JESUS

16

BIBLICAL AND THEOLOGICAL INTERPRETATIONS

THE CAYCE READINGS do not hesitate to make larger or comprehensive theological interpretations when deemed appropriate for the person or persons requesting a reading. Thus we find an attempt to summarize the Gospel, the teaching of Jesus, in the following. "Remember that the whole Gospel of Jesus Christ is, 'Thou shalt love the Lord thy God with all thy mind, thy heart, and thy body—and thy neighbor as thyself.' Do this and thou shalt have eternal life" (no. 2072–14; compare Mark 12:28–34 and parallels). We may recall that in the New Testament synoptic gospels this response of Jesus is cited as his own summation of the law of the "old dispensation," truth equally applicable to his own and every age. We may also properly note that this identification of "the whole Gospel of Jesus Christ" with Jesus' own summation of the Hebraic tradition at its best puts emphasis upon an active rather than a passive human response to divine initiative and grace.

We find in the following reading a summation of what is called "the whole duty of man": "The whole duty of man in any experience is to show forth the love the Father has shown, in the manner and in the way as to bring hope to those that—from the material things—have lost sight of the promises to the children of men" (no. 1469–1; compare Heb. 6:10–12). Let us note here again use of the term "promises," seen of course as divine promises, as summary of the meaning of the Bible as a whole.

In the course of this commentary many readings have been quoted that contain theological interpretations—usually brief—of the larger meaning of the person and work of Jesus the Christ. In this section I shall attempt to bring these into a clearer focus and order, especially by correlating readings or statements from readings that purpose to do this very thing. Let us first consider statements giving us the wider perspectives that the Cayce readings offer of the Christ event.

Reading no. 587–6 combines in a few words the cosmic ranges of the meaning of that great event and its effects in the personal lives of individuals. We note reference to "that activity [of Jesus the Christ] that *changed*, as it were, the course of the stars in their movement about the earth, and that becomes in the hearts and souls of men that hope which *quickens* as the water of life, that heals as does the kind word spoken to those that are in doubt and fear" (compare John 4:13–14; Mark 1:41; 10:13–16; Luke 12:7, 32). (As we have seen to be a common practice in the Cayce readings, this statement regarding the larger theological significance of the person and work of Jesus the Christ is immediately followed by an interpretation of its meaning that calls for comparable life activity from his followers, even as it also involves personal fellowship with him. This methodology is often undergirded by frequent quotation of the biblical principle of the solidarity, the reciprocal relationship, of the risen Christ with the whole of his creation. "For this is His teaching, 'As ye do it unto the least of my brethren, ye do it unto me' " [no. 578–6; compare Matt. 25:40; Prov. 19:17].) We also note that the birth of the Christ Child was "for *all* the peoples" (no. 1152–3; compare Luke 2:30–32).

In another reading we find the statement that "in Him is indeed the light that lightens the world" (no. 1010–12; compare John 1:9). This statement of the universal significance and effects of the person and role of the Christ, in conformity with the faith-perceptions of the prologue of the Gospel of

John, is immediately followed, however, in typical Cayce fashion, by its corollary in human application. "Only in just living His way may we indeed be like Him. Only may the awareness come in being that character of individual, with that purpose, that attitude which He manifested ever" (compare Acts 10:38), a clear call to the *imitatio Christi* (compare Phil. 2:1–11). Then we are given in brief vignette form a summary of the character of Jesus, his consistent quality of life in action. "Though He came to His own and His own received Him not, never—*never*—did He rail at them! Never did He manifest any other than just gentleness, kindness, brotherly love, patience, with those who were the most unkind" (no. 1010–12; compare John 1:11).

As a Canadian missionary friend of mine, Ian MacLeod, said more than once in my hearing in our years of service in Japan, "Jesus warned people. He never threatened them"—a good restatement, I believe, of the Cayce statement just quoted. We should note in addition that the last words in the quotation in the paragraph above may properly be referred to the apostle Paul's listing of the fruits of the Spirit in Galatians 5:22–23. The Cayce readings, in addition to frequent quotation, with minor variations, of this Pauline listing, also try to specify some of the effects in human life of the manifestation of these fruits.

They bring hope where none has been, they bring cheer where confusion has existed, they bring the longings for peace where turmoil or misunderstanding has existed—and the result becomes more and more . . . the peace that makes the heart glad, that brings the renewing of hope, that brings the understanding of joy unabated in the lives and the hearts of all that *will* come and take of the water of life freely. For the Spirit and the Bride say, "Come, and whosoever *will*, let him take of the water of life freely." (no. 1158–10; compare Rev. 22:17)

We have seen in the sections on the cross and resurrection of Jesus the Christ that the Cayce readings identify the central significance of this focus of Jesus' life, indeed of the whole of his life, as residing in its redemptive character, its meaning for others. That is, although certain aspects of this life and work were for the benefit of Jesus himself, their primary significance lay, and lies, in their value and power in furnishing both vicarious (or substitutionary) atonement—liberation of human beings from their own selves and past, or from hostile powers, that they may be reconciled with their Maker, as with each other, and be granted the opportunity to begin anew in life, to have a fresh start, even daily. Furthermore, the life and work of Jesus form a pattern, the ideal pattern, for all human life. And we have seen that the effects of that life and work of "Christ, who took upon Himself the burden of the world" (no. 262–3; compare Gal. 6: 2, 5), were and are universal in their range and scope. For this and other reasons the Cayce readings also specifically refer to Jesus as God, "For Jesus, the Christ, as God, is the same yesterday, today, and forever" (no. 1152–3; compare John 20:28–29; Heb. 13:8). (Perceptive readers may already have noticed that the theological faith-understanding manifested in the Cayce readings is especially close to the thought of the author(s) of the Johannine literature of the New Testament, as it is to that of the Letter to the Hebrews.)

At the same time the Cayce readings—without fully reconciling possible theological or logical inconsistencies—affirm that Jesus "became *indeed* the Son—through the things which He experienced in the varied planes [on earth and in supernal realms] as the development came to the oneness with the position in that which man terms the Triune" (no. 5749–3; compare Rom. 1:4). This was the result of "the development of that first entity of flesh and blood through the earth" (no. 5749–3; compare Luke 3:38; 1 Cor. 15:45–50), a Cayce affirmation of the identity of the Pauline first and second Adam. This is to say that we are here dealing with the concept of a process, from Adam—who is called son of God in the Lucan genealogy of Jesus (Luke 3:38)—to Jesus of Nazareth, a process of moral and spiritual development to the end that the entity called Jesus "became ... the Son" and thus a part of the divine Trinity. (It is well to recall that the term "Trinity" does not occur in the New Testament and appears conceptually in the creeds of the Christian church for the first time in the fourth century.) "He, through all, grew to where [the Father would say of Him], 'This is my beloved Son; hear ye Him,' for He hath the words of life" (no. 262–82; compare Mark 1:11; John 6:68). (We read elsewhere, "The soul is an individual, individuality, that may grow to be one with, or separate from, the Whole." Jesus of Nazareth is viewed in the Cayce readings as the firstborn of the souls, of the sons of God, and as the first to "grow to be one with ... the Whole" [no. 5749–3; compare Rom. 8:29; Col. 1:15].)

This emphasis upon Jesus' worthiness to be called the Son because he "developed" or "grew" to the point of manifesting fully and perfectly the life-qualities of that status is at least in part reminiscent of the emphasis of the understanding of the New Testament Letter to the Hebrews, whose author wrote of Jesus, "Although he was a Son, he learned obedience through what he suffered, and being made perfect he became the source of eternal salvation to all who obey him, being designated by God a high priest after the order of Melchizedek" (Heb. 5:8; compare Heb. 2:10; 12:2).

The apostle Paul may also have had something of the same thought in mind; such may be indicated in his use of the language of "designation," after certain conditions had been fulfilled. Thus we read at the beginning of his Letter to the Romans, "the gospel concerning his Son, who was descended from David according to the flesh and designated Son of God in power according to the Spirit of holiness by his resurrection from the dead, Jesus Christ our Lord" (Rom. 1:3–4). Paul elsewhere speaks of Jesus as "the image of the invisible God, the firstborn of all creation" (Col. 1:15; compare Rom. 8:29; Heb. 12:23). Paul's language—in both Col.

1:15 and Rom. 8:29—seems to correspond precisely with central themes of the christology of the Cayce readings.

This then is the background of faith-understanding for the many statements in the Edgar Cayce readings that emphasize the uniqueness of Jesus' person, status, and role in God's universe. Repeatedly we read, "He is the Way, He is the Truth, the Light, and no other name is given under heaven whereby man may be made whole, or whereby man may know his true relationships to God" (no. 1152–3; compare John 14:6; Acts 4:12). As we have already seen, this kind of statement in the Cayce readings, even as it depends upon the New Testament itself, is not to be understood in a mechanical way, as if verbal repetition of a name, or any other external performance, constitutes an authentic and effective religious activity apart from corresponding interiority of persons. In its main thrust the Bible itself, both Old Testament and New, with its Hebraic usage of the "name" as designative of the whole person, forthrightly rejects such an interpretation.

This Cayce affirmation (quoting John 14:6 and Acts 4:12) is also not to be understood in an exclusive way, as if failure to pronounce the name of Jesus verbally removes persons from the possibility of ultimate salvation. That was not, for example, the intention of the author of the Acts of the Apostles, nor probably of the apostle Peter, who is quoted as saying later in the same book, "Truly I perceive that God shows no partiality, but in every nation any one who fears him [God] and does what is right is acceptable to him" (Acts 10: 34–35; compare Acts 14:15–17; 17:24–30).

The Cayce readings insist in the same vein that "God calls on man everywhere to seek His face, through that channel that may be blessed by the Spirit of the Son—in whatsoever sphere this may take its form" (no. 364–9). This language seems clearly to mean that the living God, "the Father of our Lord Jesus Christ," is present and at work throughout the whole of his creation. It means also that the Son is also participant in this "wider work of God in the world" and that he may work through, "bless," a variety of spiritual channels even though they may not bear the name Christian. The Cayce statement also means that to every human being some such spiritual channel is available, a channel—presumably religious personages and traditions are primarily indicated by this language, but other personal and cultural influences may assuredly not be excluded—through which God addresses every human being and within which he uses his Son to "bless," that is, to purify, correct, and enhance that same channel. It is in this context of understanding that we are to read the frequent Cayce statement that "There's only one Master" (no. 3545–1) and "there *is* a light in Israel" (no. 774–5). The implications of this faith-understanding for Christian theology, if taken seriously as the true meaning of Scripture, are significant indeed.

We also read, "Know today there is no other than that found in the admonition given by Jesus of Nazareth, Jesus the Christ—'If ye believe in God, believe also in me' " (no. 2629–1; compare John 14:1). Here, as often elsewhere, the Cayce readings take up the Johannine thesis that it is our human responsibility to accept the one(s) whom God the Father sends (compare John 6:29; Mark 12:1–12, and parallels). Jesus, furthermore, is said to be "*the* only one; for, as He gave, 'He that climbs up any other way is a thief and a robber. . . . there *is only* one" (no. 364–9; compare John 10:1). The meaning of this Cayce interpretive quotation of the Johannine verse seems to be that, while there is a distinctive uniqueness in the person and role of Jesus of Nazareth, the emphasis appears to be on the distinctiveness of the way characteristic of Jesus. And, as we have seen, this same Jesus, either as preexistent Logos or as risen Christ, presides over a wider availability and practice of his way than has been commonly perceived in most Western theological traditions until very recent years.

The Cayce readings have a further distinction to make. "CHRIST is not a man! *Jesus* was the man, Christ the messenger, Christ in all ages, Jesus in one, Joshua in another, Melchizedek in another" (no. 991–1). This language admittedly seems to differ from that of the Gospel of John, where we read, "And the Word became flesh and dwelt among us" (John 1:14), language that has historically been taken to mean a literal incarnation of the divine Logos, with no distinction of person implied. The Cayce mode of speech seems to imply a spiritual indwelling and an ontological distinction of some kind between the Logos and the man Jesus. (Rudolf Steiner seems to have such a perception of the relationship between the divine Logos and Jesus of Nazareth when he writes in *The Gospel of St. Luke* that the "Christ, or the Logos, was incarnated in the man, Jesus of Nazareth, who experienced inwardly "the Logos in its complete original form."")

One Cayce reading speaks of the Christ (the Logos) as "taking up the life of the man Jesus" to the end that his life became "life in glory" (no. 5749–4). This mode of expression seems to be connected elsewhere with Jesus' baptism and transfiguration experiences, when he received "those acknowledgements of the Father that he *was* the one who could, *would*, through those activities, become the Savior of man" (no. 262–29; compare Mark 1:9–11; 9:7). This language, however, in the context of the Edgar Cayce readings does not mean displacement of personhood. The readings consistently assume the ongoing operation of Jesus' personal consciousness and will. They seem to apply also to Jesus the following description that can be used of all people who open self to relationship with their Creator in full self-awareness: "the individual entity opening the consciousness of self to that abiding Presence" whereby "that Light enters" (no. 2533–8). The result is spiritual communion in full and willing personal consciousness, with harmony of purpose and will, union of spirit, cooperation in work. This result was achieved perfectly in the case of Jesus. With others on the earth plane the process remains incomplete.

The Cayce readings do not put Jesus, Joshua, and Melchizedek all on precisely the same level. The soul entity is seen as the same, but, on the basis of the moral and spiritual development noted above, there is a perfection of union of Jesus and the Christ that does not obtain comparably in the other cases. And, given the high anthropology expressed in the Cayce readings—even more, the very high view of the entity who became Adam and then Jesus of Nazareth—ontological discontinuity between the man Jesus and the Universal Logos is not as sharply perceived as in some traditional or contemporary christological formulations. In any case, the readings contend that the union which issued in Jesus the Christ made possible cosmically effective divine-human activity for the full redemption and ultimate salvation of all humanity that had not been possible in any other way or through any other historical or transhistorical persons.

We have, however, already noted statements in the Cayce readings, suggesting that this high christology, this view of the cosmic uniqueness of the person and work of Jesus the Christ, is to be understood in such a way as to assign to personages and movements outside the Judeo-Christian tradition their own significance under God. That is, the readings give appropriate, and in certain cases not a little, value and meaning to these activities as within the larger saving work of God in the world, a work that theologians—often with much narrower scope of meaning—have called the history of salvation. For example, even though the work for others of Jesus in his previous incarnations is not to be considered as precisely the same in kind or degree as that in his role as Jesus of Nazareth, it is said that he "influenced either directly or indirectly all those forms of philosophy or religious thought that taught that God was One" (no. 364–9). The same reading says that this entity who became Jesus "associated with—in the meditation or spirit of" Gautama the Buddha. These two quotations, when taken together, should be understood, I believe, on the basis that the Buddha's faith-object, the Dharma, was perceived by him as unitive and supreme to the extent that we may rightly include him in the category of those who taught that God is one. (For my own views of the larger issues relating to the Buddha and the

Christ, readers are invited to consult my *Gautama the Buddha, An Essay in Religious Understanding*.)

Furthermore, the point is made that in subsequent historical developments in Judaism, Hinduism, Buddhism, Confucianism, Platonism, and Islam, there has "been added . . . much from that as was given by Jesus in His walk in Galilee and Judea" (no. 364–9). This language can of course be understood as meaning the influence of Jesus upon these other religious developments as operative solely on the historical plane. But the Cayce readings, here and elsewhere, seem to indicate that the influence works also from supernal planes, from the work of the risen Christ. They affirm that as an accessible and working Reality "in all these, then, there is that same impelling Spirit" (no. 364–9).

The Cayce readings do not intend, of course, to give uncritical or blanket approval to all that has been said and done in these historical movements, any more than they would to the totality of the movement called Christianity. We find in fact discriminating appreciation. Specifically we are told that the historical founders or subsequent leaders of these movements "are as teachers or representatives" to be duly respected but not to be considered fully comparable, in either person or role, with the Master, Jesus the Christ—even though "the Spirit of the Master, the Spirit of the Son, was manifest—as was given—to each in their respective sphere . . . for, as has been given, there is *only* one—the others are as those acting in the capacity of the thought that was given to them through that same Power, that 'In the last days has He spoken unto us through the Son, as one born out of due season' " (no. 364–9; compare Heb. 1:1; 1 Cor. 15:8).

The other great figures of humanity's spiritual pilgrimage have been but as "stepping stones" to the higher knowledge of the Son of God in the lives of human beings. In Jesus the Christ is found the supreme Advocate with the Father (no. 262–14; compare 1 John 2:1). Thus we are told, "Pray rather to the Son, the Father through the Son, that He walks with thee—and He *will* walk and talk with thee. Be *not* satisfied with ANY other . . . *He* is the Way; there is no other" (no. 5749–4; compare John 14:6). "The Christ is the Son, the way *to* the Father, and One that came into the earth as man, the Son of man, that man might have access to the Father, hence the way" (no. 262–28; compare Rom. 5:1–2; Eph. 2: 18; 3:12).

This reading in the same context speaks also of Michael as "an archangel that stands before the throne of the Father . . . Michael is the lord or the guard of the change that comes in every soul that seeks the way, even as in those periods when His [the Christ's] manifestations came in the earth" (no. 262–28). We may note that the language here seems closer to the faith-understanding of John 1:14, "And the Word became flesh and dwelt among us, full of grace and truth; we have beheld his glory, glory as of the only Son from the Father."

In sum, the Cayce readings speak of "Jesus the Christ . . . to whom all honor and all glory are due" (no. 1158–5). "Jesus *is* the one who was promised from that day [when the Lord God said to Eve], 'and her seed shall bruise his [the serpent's] head' " (no. 2067–1; compare Gen. 3:15). This is all to say that Jesus the Christ is the central figure in the universal history of divine salvation.

INTERPRETATIONS

At this point it would be well to attempt to place the theological interpretations of Jesus the Christ found in the Edgar Cayce readings within their larger views of God and the cosmos. From there we shall move on to a broad survey of the interpretations themselves that will, I hope, constitute at least a partial recapitulation of all that has gone before in this book.

The Cayce readings affirm that "in the beginning God moved and mind, knowledge, came into being—and the earth and the fulness thereof became the result of same" (no.

5000–1; compare Gen. 1:1–2:24; 5:1–2). We have already noted the similarities of this Cayce cosmological perception with the Upanishadic views of ancient India. Correlations also appear with recent speculations of astrophysics and astrobiology (see Lyall Watson's *Beyond Supernature* for more on this subject). "God moved and said, 'Let there be light,' and there was light, not the light of the sun, but rather that of which, through which, in which every soul had, has and ever has its being. For in truth ye live and move and have thy being in Him" (no. 5246–1; see also no. 3508–1; compare Gen. 1:1, 3; John 1:4–5, 9; 8:1; Acts 17:28).

God is described as Universal Consciousness (no. 2823–1). He is "that which is everlasting, which is and can be only constructive" (no. 1493–1). God is also perceived as "good" (no. 1580–1; compare Mark 10:18 and parallels); as "all-inclusive love" (no. 2110–1; compare 1 John 4:16); love which was manifested in a uniquely pure way by Jesus the Christ, he "who took upon Himself the burdens of the world" (no. 2110–1; see also no. 1497–1; compare Matt. 11: 28–30). This manifestation of divine love by Jesus, however, lies not only in Jesus' expression on earth of the same quality of love as the Father's, but especially in the fact that the entire life-event constituted by Christ Jesus is the consequence of activity of the Father, for "God so loved the world as to give—*give*—His only begotten Son, who took on the form of flesh that He might know the manner of man's experience in the earth" (no. 276–2; compare John 3:16; 5: 17, 19, 30; 6:37, 44; Phil. 2:5–7). Jesus is "the very gift" of the Father (no. 1504–1). The Father's love is infinite (no. 1158–14; compare Matt. 5:45); Jesus the Christ *is, was*, and "EVER WILL BE the expression, the *concrete* expression" of that love (no. 696–3; compare 1 John 1:1–2). Jesus is "the manifested love of an All-Wise, All-Merciful Father" (no. 823–1), and because he is risen and therefore universally available,

No soul has been left without that access to the throne of mercy and grace through which each soul—as the promise has been given—may be at-one with those Creative Forces that are found in Him who has given, "If ye love me ye will keep my commandments, and I will come and abide with thee," and ye shall have peace in thine inner self that passeth understanding to those that know Him not. (no. 823–1; compare John 10:30; 14:15, 18, 27; 17:21; Phil. 4:7)

In the Edgar Cayce readings the Godhead is frequently described as triune: "The Godhead is the Father, the Son, the Holy Spirit" (no. 1348–1; compare 2 Cor. 13:14). We are informed in some measure of the interrelationship between the "Members" of the Trinity in the statement that the ideal mode of human cooperation is "just as in Father, Son, and Holy Spirit" (no. 2396–2). Thus the three "Parts" of the Trinity are een as somehow "personal," but "the Father, the Son, and the Holy Spirit are One" (no. 1597–1; compare John 10:30; 1 Cor. 12:11; Gal. 3:20).

As we have seen, the basic oneness of God is a central thesis of the Cayce readings (compare Mark 12:29 and parallels). This faith-understanding, however, like that of the Christian creeds of the fourth century, posits a oneness capable of bearing distinctions within it, "capable of manifestation in the varied planes of development" (no. 5749–3), with the term "individual entity" even being used of each "Member" of the Trinity. The relationship within human beings of our body, mind, and soul (or spirit) is frequently used in the readings to indicate this combination of oneness and distinction within the Divine Trinity (no. 1597–1; no. 1348–1; no. 2559–1).

We find, however, the further assertion that with such trinitarian language we are expressing human concepts, that "man's concept of the Godhead is three-dimensional—Father, Son and Holy Spirit" (no. 4035–1). This is not to say that the concept of God as triune has no relationship to reality. It is rather to be seen as the human perception of the Godhead as this is humanly comprehensible in a three-dimensional world. We are here able to perceive the Godhead as "three-dimensional activity in a three-dimensional world" (no. 2283–1), the components of which are frequently cited in the Cayce readings as "time, space, and patience" (no. 4035–1).

Thus it is asserted that since human beings—our souls— potentially "may think in an eight-dimensional consciousness, . . . the Universal Consciousness manifested or expressed in the three-dimensional as Father, Son and Holy Spirit . . . might be manifested or indicated in many more" dimensions in other realms than on earth (no. 3037–1; see also no. 3188–1). This is to say no more than sensitive theologians have long been saying, namely, that God is more than our human theologies are able adequately to describe (compare Rom. 11:33–36).

The Cayce readings, we may add, occasionally make reference to the vastness of the cosmos, to "the other chambers of God's universe," to the fact that "we pass from one room to another, from one consciousness to another," and that these stages of consciousness are "but stepping-stones to the greater consciousness which He [God the Father] would have each soul attain in its relationships with and usage of its fellow men" (no. 2282–1). With reference to the placement and relationship of this planet earth to the larger whole, we are told that "the earth is that speck, that part in creation where souls [previously created] projected themselves into matter" (no. 5755–2). "The earth is only an atom in the universe of worlds!" (no. 5749–3).

A primary theological issue emerges, however, as to the nature of the relationship of Jesus of Nazareth to the Divine Trinity, for "In the beginning was the Word, and that Spirit, that Christ Spirit *was* the Word" (no. 524–2; compare John 1:1). The emphasis of the Cayce readings is that Jesus "became the Son" and can therefore be called God. A question, however, naturally arises whether there was a "time" when the soul-entity who became Jesus of Nazareth and came, rightly, to be called the Christ, the Son of God, was not a part of the Trinity.

The answer is both yes and no—not in the sense of evasive equivocation, but because the perceptions of the Cayce readings involve subtleties of distinction that have not often been taken seriously in recent centuries but may be traced in various theological streams in the early Christian church. Yes, in the sense that this soul-entity was created, both in the primal sense of creation as the first man, as we now know human beings in earthly and historical experience (no. 1158–5; no. 2072–4; no. 5749–3; compare Gen. 1:27; 5:1–2). Yet even with this affirmation of Jesus' belonging to the created order, the Cayce readings consistently insist upon a uniqueness. "That entity, that *soul* called Jesus . . . is . . . the only-begotten, the firstborn, the first to know flesh, the first to purify it" (no. 1158–5), a theme that the readings share particularly with the New Testament authors of the Letter to the Colossians and of the Revelation to John. It is significantly also a theme of the apostle Paul's major Letter to the Romans (compare Rom. 8:29; Col. 1:15; Rev. 3:14). Not only is Jesus "the Elder Brother to all who are *born* in the earth" (no. 1158–5; compare Matt. 28:10; Rom. 8:29; Heb. 2:11–12, 17), but he is also known "as the Maker, the Creator, as the first, as the last, as the beginning, as the end of man's soul experience through the earth and throughout the spheres of consciousness in and about the earth" (no. 1158–5; compare Rev. 22:13). Jesus is the Son of man *par excellence* and therefore is also "the Son of God, the Son of the First Cause, making manifest in a material body" (no. 5749–3; compare 1 John 1:2). The Cayce perception of Jesus, who became the Christ, as somehow also participating in the activity of divine creation is another theme shared with New Testament writers (compare John 1:1–3, 10, 14; 1 Cor. 8:6; Col. 1:16; Heb. 1:2).

Yet the answer to the preceding question is also no. For Jesus is said to be "a part of the Creator" from the beginning (no. 2072–4); "the portion of God that manifests" (no.

1158–5; compare John 1:18; 1 Tim. 3:16; 1 John 1:2). This conclusion is at least in part possible because of the high view of humanity in the Cayce readings, that "each soul is a son of God" (no. 5252–1; compare Luke 3:38; John 10: 31–39; Ps. 82:6). Another reading says that "each soul—not the body but the soul—is the image of the Maker" (no. 2246–1; compare Gen. 1:27; 5:1). We are "the offspring of the Creative Forces," created to be companions therewith (no. 2428–1; compare Acts 17:28–29; John 15:15; Luke 12: 4). "The soul of each individual is a portion then of the Whole, *with* the birthright of Creative Forces to become a co-creator with the Father, a co-laborer with Him" (no. 1549–1; compare 2 Cor. 6:1) and thus "a channel of blessing to others" (no. 3161–1; compare Rom. 15:29). The distinction, between soul and body, frequently found, does not mean that the Cayce readings ever disparage the human physical body. Quite the contrary: They share and emphasize with the apostle Paul the faith-understanding that the body is the temple of the living God (no. 262–10, 29, 67, 82, 86, 87, 89; compare 1 Cor. 3:16–17; 6:15, 19; 2 Cor. 6:16).

But this statement is immediately followed, in the same reading, with the addition, "but He was the first, the light, the way, the truth, the high priest of the soul of men, the brother in mind and body, that we as individuals might know the Father-God" (no. 5252–1; compare Rev. 1:8; 21:6; 22: 13; John 1:4, 9; 8:12; 14:6; Heb. 3:1; and so on). The Cayce readings thus in effect tell us that Jesus was both God and man from the beginning, but that as man he became the perfect man and, as such, the perfect instrument of the Father for the redemption and full salvation of all humanity, indeed for the restoration of the entire cosmos.

TRUTH UNTO GOODNESS

The reasons in the larger cosmic situation for Jesus' becoming the Christ are given in considerable abundance, but it is necessary to recall that in the Cayce readings preexistence is affirmed not only of Jesus. All souls are said to have preexisted from the beginning of creation: "All souls in the beginning were one with the Father. The separation, or turning away, brought evil" (no. 262–56; compare Gen. 3:1–24). In the Cayce readings this "separation" does not denote an ontological phenomenon—as though the fact of consciousness distinct from the Creator's, or creation itself, intrinsically constituted evil. It indicates rather a primarily ethical phenomenon, wrought by possessors of free will, therefore a "turning away."

We may recall that in the Cayce readings, as in the Bible as a whole, the essence of evil is seen as the rupture of personal relationships, first (in theological priority, not necessarily temporal) with our Maker and then with each other. The essence of salvation is the restoration of personal relationships in the same order, the reconciliation of persons. The readings emphasize in the strongest way, and repeatedly, that human beings—as souls—have been given free will as a birthright by their Creator (no. 262–15, 52, 63, 64, 85). And the Father has willed from the beginning that no soul should perish (no. 262–85; no. 1663–2; no. 2081–1; no. 3581–1; compare 1 Tim. 2:4; 4:10; 2 Pet. 3:9). In order that every individual entity should "in peace, in harmony, build those purposes whereunto it has been called, or whereunto the Spirit of Truth has purposed in an entity's consciousness" (no. 2812–1; compare 1 Cor. 1:9; Gal. 5:13; Eph. 4:1–16; Col. 3:15; 1 Tim. 6:12; 1 Pet. 2:21), God has prepared the way, of which we find the culmination in Jesus the Christ (1458–1; 2397–1; 417–8; compare 1 Cor. 10:13).

According to the Cayce readings there are various aspects and a variety of meanings in the Christ event when seen in the large. On the one hand

As man found himself out of touch with that complete consciousness of the oneness of God, it became necessary that the will of God the Father be made manifested, that a pattern be introduced into man's consciousness. Thus the Son of man came into the earth, made in the form, the likeness of man, with body, mind, soul. Yet the soul was the Son, the soul was the Light. (no. 3357–2; compare Phil. 2:1–11)

This is to affirm the role of Jesus in providing the perfect pattern of God's will and also to say that the soul of Jesus was indeed one with the Second Person of the Divine Trinity, the primal Light.

On the other hand, in the same passage we read of the specifically redemptive aspect of Jesus' work, his liberating, reconciling, restorative work for others. "For all men (and He was a man) have fallen short of the glory of God. Only in Him, through Him, by Him may one attain to that true relationship, that true fellowship, that true relationship to the Creative Forces or God" (no. 3357–2; compare Rom. 8:15; Gal. 4:4–7; 1 John 1:1–3). Jesus of Nazareth is "that One that has been given into the world to become the Savior, the Redeemer of the world" (no. 413–3; compare John 4:42; Tit. 1:4; 2 Pet. 1:1; 1 John 4:14).

Thus the work of Jesus the Christ represents the will and action both of the Father and of Jesus himself. The same will and action, however, are to become ours.

The Christ Consciousness in the earth was manifested through the lowly Nazarene, that came in order that man—through His example, His love, His patience, His hope manifested, through the attributes of the Spirit that He exemplified in His activity both as to word and as to precept—might choose, as He, to do that which is right, that which is just, that which is sincere, that which is honest in the activities one with another. (no. 272–9; compare Acts 10:38; 1 Cor. 13:4–13; Gal. 5: 22–23; Phil. 4:8)

"The Christ Child was born into the earth as man, one born in due season, in due time, in man's spiritual evolution, that man might have a pattern of the personality and individuality of God Himself" (no. 5758–1; compare Gal. 4:1–11; Col. 1:15; Heb. 1:1–3; Phil. 2:5; 1 Tim. 1:16). This role of Christ Jesus as pattern or model for all humanity, even as he faithfully, indeed perfectly, represents the character of the Creator himself, looms large in the Cayce readings. The perception, too, that the time of his coming was providentially ordered, appropriate to human need at the right time in the spiritual evolution of humanity, is in accord of course with New Testament apostolic faith-understanding. This same reading also affirms the redemptive, restorative role of the Christ in saying, "Ye have been justified once for all, through the Christ Consciousness that ye seek" (no. 5758–1; Heb. 7:27; 9:26–27; 10:10; 1 Pet. 3:18). This is the universal Christ Consciousness, the Universal Consciousness of the Father, with which Jesus of Nazareth was in perfect union.

But that there be no misunderstanding, that we human beings may then assume our own responsibilities in God's universal saving program, the same reading goes on to say, "Each individual must do unto others as he would have his brother, the Christ, his God, the Father do unto him; and then apply first, last and always His 'Forgive, O God, as I forgive others. Find fault in me, O God, as I find fault in my brother' " (no. 5758–1; compare Matt. 7:12; 6:14–15). We have already noted this teaching under the rubric of the principle of reciprocity as of solidarity. The Cayce readings are equal to any Protestant conservative evangelical in their strong emphasis upon the theological priority of God's love and grace in action, supremely manifested in Jesus the Christ. No one can earn or merit the love of God; we cannot earn or merit the love of our fellow human beings. There is always something extra, generous, free, mysterious in authentic love.

But the readings will not let us forget the so-called "hard

sayings" of the New Testament, specifically of the teaching of Jesus. One instance is the Gospel of Matthew's version of the Lord's Prayer, in which Jesus chooses to emphasize by repetition only one element of the prayer, "For if you forgive men their trespasses, your heavenly Father also will forgive you; but if you do not forgive men their trespasses, neither will your Father forgive your trespasses" (Matt. 6: 14–15). The Cayce readings would have us remember this warning and forgive, even "seventy-times seven" (Matt. 18: 22).

The Cayce readings, however, also portray the larger picture, in saying that Christ Jesus "came into the earth that we through Him might have eternal life" (no. 1747–5; compare John 3:16). This same grand truth is expressed elsewhere in even more tellingly personal language, where we read that he put on flesh "that He might become the way through which man might find his way home—*home*" (no. 849–18; compare John 14:1–6; Luke 15:11–32). Another reading speaks of "the way of the cross that leads home" (no. 3347–1; compare Mark 8:34–35 and parallels). The cosmic significance of the Christ event is emphasized by seeing "God as manifested in the Christ Child" (no. 849–18).

This cosmic perspective, the wide-ranging cosmic aspects of the Christ event, are brought into a personal focus of helpful comfort in a reading addressed to a thirty-year-old woman, "Did not the Son of man descend even from the presence of the Father into the earth, and then into hell itself, that . . . all might know He walks and talks with thee, my child, if ye will but listen to the voice from within" (no. 295–9; no. 262–75; compare Eph. 4:8–10; 1 Pet. 3:18–19; 4:6; 1 Kings 19:12–13). This ancient Christian theme of the *Descensus ad Inferos*, the descent of the risen Christ into hell for redemptive purposes, a theme that continues to be affirmed in Christian worship across the world in the recitation of the Apostles' Creed, plays a significant role in the perceptions of the Cayce readings regarding the work of Jesus the Christ. For Rudolf Steiner also the Descent into Hell was "an event of a spiritual nature that really occurred." At the same time the application of this theological grandeur—as hopeful as it is grand—is given personal focus in a very large number of readings by emphasis upon the importance of listening to "the voice from within," "a still small voice" (1 Kings 19:12–13), a method of communication that the risen Christ still deigns to use to those who will hear and heed.

Regarding, again, the larger theological posture, many readings refer to or paraphrase the famous passage in the apostle Paul's Letter to the Philippians. This is Paul writing toward the end of his life, Paul at the most mature and mellow stage of his Christian faith. One reading, addressed to Edgar Cayce personally, speaks of "Jesus the Christ . . . who made His life of *no* estate, that others might *know* the love and the Fatherhood of God, that He, the Christ, might become the Living Way, the Approach to the Father" (no. 294–71; compare Phil. 2:1–11; Rom. 5:1–2; Eph. 2:17–18; 3:11–12). Elsewhere we read that the Christ "thought it not robbery to make Himself equal with God, yet put on flesh" (no. 849–18; compare Phil. 2:1–11).

There are frequent references in the Cayce readings to Jesus' role as Christus Victor, victor over the forces of evil of every kind, manifesting in any form, on the earth or in supernal realms. These forces are also spoken of as specifically being obstacles to the good life of human beings. Thus we read that "He manifested in flesh that the evil forces, as manifest in the relationships of individuals as one to another, may be eradicated from the experience of man" (no. 1293–1; compare John 17:15; Gal. 1:4; 7 Pet. 1:3–5). "He overcame the flesh, the death, and evil—the devil. . . . He passed through the garden, the cross, the grave, hell, and rose in the *newness* of all being put *under* submission. For having overcome He *became* the Way, the Light, the Savior" (no. 288–30; compare Luke 11:19–23; John 16:33; Eph. 4:8; Rev. 13:10; 1 John 5:4–5; Rev. 12:10–11; 17:14). And because Christ Jesus overcame, we, too, by abiding in him "may overcome the world also" (no. 3051–2; see also no. 3508–1; compare

John 15:5; 16:33; 17:15). Elsewhere we read that he "over-came sin, error, dis-ease, disease and even death itself in the material plane" (no. 479–1; compare Rom. 5:12–21; 6:9–11).

It is specifically said in the Cayce readings that "In the *cross* He *became* the Savior . . . In the *cross* He overcame" (no. 793–2). But the background of the event of the cross and the basis of Jesus' overcoming was his "surrendering all power unto Power itself, surrendering all will unto the will of the Father, making of self then a channel" (no. 1152–1; compare Mark 14:36, 39 and parallels, Phil. 2:7–8). This reading goes on to suggest that frequent use of the prayer, "Thy will, O God, not mine, but Thine, be done in me, through me," can facilitate a proper application by human beings of this spirit of self-surrender to the Father. This prayer is cited as the prayer of Jesus and also of all who would know "a cleansing of the body, of the flesh, of the blood, in such measures that it may may become illumined with power from on high" (no. 1152–1).

While Jesus' experience of the cross was the focus of his entire life, it was in a profound sense spiritually representative, in its quality of full surrender of his will to God the Father, of the whole of that life. Thus we read,

> Though He were the Son, yet learned He obedience through the things that that He suffered. He used, then, that which was necessary in the experience in the earth as periods of suffering, as periods of rejection, even by His own that He had called, that were His friends— not as stumbling-stones but as stepping-stones to make for thee, for the world, that access for each soul, for the closer relationship of the Father, through the Son, to the children of men. (no. 2600–2; compare Heb. 5: 8; John 1:11; Matt. 26:50)

Elsewhere we find, "He has attained the Christ Conscious-ness in giving of Himself. Though able in mental and physical to lay aside the cross, He accepted same, offering self as the sacrifice, that ye might have an Advocate in the Father. Thus are ye saved, by grace" (no. 3459–1; compare Matt. 26:53–54; Eph. 5:2; Heb. 9:26; 10:12; 1 John 2:1–2; Eph. 2: 8). "For the blood as of the perfect man was shed . . . that there might be made an offering once for all" (no. 1504–1; compare Heb. 7:27). His sacrifice was in faith, that it may be counted to thee as righteousness" (no. 683–2; compare Rom. 5:17; Phil. 3:9). "He, the Christ, stands in self's stead" (no. 288–36).

The word "ransom" used in the New Testament is also found in the Cayce readings to denote the nature and effect of the work of Jesus the Christ. It refers specifically to the effective power of "the love He showed in *giving* Himself as the ransom for many" (no. 347–2; compare Mark 10:45; Mt. 20:28; 1 Tim. 2:5–6). "He himself paid . . ." (no. 3213– 2; compare 1 Cor. 6:20; 7:23). The relationship of the person and work of Christ Jesus to the "older dispensation" and, again, their proper effects in the lives of believers is beautifully expressed in the following reading.

As the law of sacrifice as committed unto man bespoke the coming of the law of mercy that was and is demonstrated in the life of the man Jesus, thy Christ, who offered Himself as the sacrifice once for all, entering into the Holy of Holies where He may meet thee day by day, thou art then indeed—as many as have named the name—come under the law of mercy, not of sacrifice. This is not in the term that no man offers sacrifice, for the life of every soul that seeks in the material world to demonstrate the spiritual life is a life of sacrifice *from* the material angle. But to such that have passed from death unto life, in that law of mercy in naming Him as thine God, thine Brother, thine Savior, who has paid, who has offered Himself, thou art passed from death unto life—and the sacrifice is as mercy from thy God to thy brother. Hence he that

would despitefully use thee, a kind word is as mercy.
As ye would have mercy, show mercy. (no. 262–72;
compare Heb. 9:11–12; Matt. 9:13; 12:7; 23:23; Hos.
6:6; John 5:24; Matt. 5:44)

The "spirit of Him who gave Himself as a ransom for
many" is described as "making self of low estate, as is
called in man's realm. All-powerful—yet never using that
power save to help, to assist, to give aid, to give succor to
someone who is not in that position to help or aid self" (no.
900–147; compare Phil. 2:5–8). Because Jesus gave himself
to the Father as a ransom, "Each soul . . . might know that
it has an Advocate *with* the Father" (no. 524–2; compare 1
John 2:1). This is supremely to the end that through Jesus
the Christ we may all be reconciled with God the Father, for,
"In the day that ye accept Him as thy sacrifice and *live*
thyself according to His precepts, *ye* become reconciled—
through Him—to the Father, and He, too, walketh and talk-
eth with thee" (no. 2879–1; compare 2 Cor. 5:18–19; Matt.
7:21). Thus, in the reciprocal Cayce fashion, our reconciliation with the Father of us all—from our condition of alien-
ation, estrangement—is seen as based on the work of Jesus
the Christ, but this same work, mightily effective in itself, is
not perceived as working automatically or mechanically in
human life. Without human cooperation it is not truly effective (compare Phil. 2:12–13).

APPLICATIONS PERSONAL AND
PARTICULAR

We are now in a position to move, so to speak, from the
cosmic to the more particular, contemporary and "practical." For Jesus the Christ as our Mediator (no. 357–13; no.
2796–1; compare 1 Tim. 2:5; Heb. 8:6; 9:15) and Advocate
(compare 1 John 2:1) is also "the answer to every problem
in material existence" (no. 1981–1; compare 1 Pet. 5:7).

"With every disturbing factor, with every ill, with every way, there has been prepared a manner, a means, a way of escape *in* Him" (no. 540–3; compare 1 Cor. 10:13). "For this experience of every soul in the material plane is not mere chance" (no. 1786–1; Matt. 10:29–31).

> For to each soul is given that which if applied in the daily life will make that soul one with the Infinite. But keep humble, keep patient, keep in the manner in which the pattern has been given. For it is even as that one manifested in the flesh, even Jesus who became the Christ, who offered Himself that ye through belief, through faith, through the pattern of His life, might find thy way . . . might find thy true relationship to the Creator, God. And He will not withhold any good thing from thee. (no. 3660–1; compare 1 John 4:2; Rom. 8: 28, 32)

These sentences give some indication of the extensive material in the Cayce readings indicative and descriptive of the Providence of God. The point to be emphasized here, however, is the claim of the total sufficiency of that Providence, of God at work in the world—both in himself and through his agents, supremely through Jesus the Christ—for *all* human needs and predicaments. The forthright affirmation is made that "all problems may be met in Him" (no. 288–36; compare 2 Cor. 12:9). Jesus' promise is, "If ye will love me, believing I am able, I will deliver thee from that which besets thee at *any* experience" (no. 987–4; compare 2 Thess. 3:3; Phil. 4:7; Rom. 8:28). "Be not afraid, for He will be thy Guide, if ye seek His face" (no. 2851–1; compare John 14: 1, 26; 16:13).

These promises lead naturally in the Cayce readings to a new focus upon prayer, as upon meditation. Both words are defined on various occasions with considerable richness of meaning, but one simple definition given is, "Prayer is supplication to God and meditation is listening to His answer" (no. 2946–6). Another is, "Prayer, in short, is appealing to the Divine within self, the Divine from without self, and meditation is keeping still in body, in mind, in heart, listening, listening to the voice of the Maker" (no. 5368–1).

A dimension of prayer central to the Cayce readings is seen in the following definition:

> Prayer is the concerted effort of the physical consciousness to become attuned to the consciousness of the Creator, either collectively or individually. *Meditation* is *emptying* self of all that hinders the Creative Forces from rising along the channels of the natural man . . . In entering into the silence, entering into the silence in meditation, with a clean hand, a clean body, a clean mind, we may receive that strength and power that fits each individual, each soul, for a greater activity in this material world. (no. 281–3; compare 1 Kings 19:8; Ps. 24:3–6)

Rather than a passive approach to life's problems and challenges, the Cayce reading forthrightly states that one should be

> constant in prayer—knowing and taking, knowing and understanding that he that is faithful is not given a burden beyond that he is able to bear, if he will put the burden upon Him that has given the promise, "I will be *with* thee; there shall not come that which shall harm thee; if thou will but put thy trust, thy faith in me." (no. 290–1; compare 1 Thess. 5:17; 1 Cor. 10:13; Matt. 11:28–30; 1 Pet. 5:7; Mark 16:18)

In language reminiscent of the older Protestant evangelicalism, we are told, "Take it to Jesus! He *is* thy answer. He is Life, Light, and Immortality. He is Truth and is thy Elder Brother" (no. 1326–1; 2 Tim. 1:10; John 14:6; Heb. 2:11). (In this same reading we find approving use of the phrase well known to readers of the American classic religious novel *In His Steps*, by Charles Monroe Sheldon, "What would Jesus have me do?" The reading insists that this question—rather than "What shall I do?"—should be asked of oneself regarding all matters "in thy relationships with thy fellow man, in thy home, in thy problems, day by day" (no. 1326–1; see also no. 288–36].) "His grace is sufficient—and has been the stay. Hold fast to that, for *that* is good" (no. 513–2; compare 2 Cor. 12:9; 1 Thess. 5:21).

We are told that the Lord God "is mindful of the prayers of the children of men" (no. 845–6; compare Ps. 102:17; Matt. 6:8). Therefore the promise, is " 'What thou asketh in *my name, believing*, ye shall have. If ye love me, keep my commandments, and I will come and dwell in thine own heart.' That is, 'I will so *fill* your mind, your *mental forces with the good*, until all else shall be driven away' " (no. 294–71; compare Matt. 21:22; John 14:13–17). " 'I will be with thee *always*,' if ye seek" (no. 1877–1; compare Matt. 28:20; 7:7–8). In this connection of filling our minds with the good, it would be well to cite a Cayce recommendation of a useful focus in Bible reading, as an accompaniment of prayer and meditation.

Meditate, pray, read the Scriptures—these particularly, the 30th of Deuteronomy, the first seven verses of the 6th of Joshua, the 23rd Psalm, the 1st Psalm, the 24th Psalm, the 150th Psalm, and know John 14, 15, 16, 17—not merely by heart, as rote, but as the law, the love, the grace, the mercy, the truth that is expressed there. For as He has given, "The earth, the heavens will pass away, but my words shall *not* pass away." (no. 1376–1; compare Mark 13:31 and parallels)

With regard to the essence of the content of the Bible, the following reading first quotes Jesus' teaching that we have already seen as his summation of the law of God for Israel—and for all: "To love the Lord with all thy heart, thy mind, thy body, and thy neighbor as thyself'' (compare Mark 12: 28–34 and parallels). The reading goes on to say, ''This is the whole will of the Father to His children. The rest of that recorded in Holy Writ—as may be said by man in his relationships, in meeting the problems every day, every age, every experience—is merely the attempt to explain, to analyze, to justify or to meet that saying, that truth'' (no. 2524–3).

In this context of emphasis upon the primary relationships and ethical principles that are said by Jesus to express the will of the Father, we note: ''He set no rule of ethics, other than 'As ye would that men should do to you, do ye even so to them,' and to know 'Inasmuch as ye do it unto the least of these thy brethren, ye do it unto thy Maker' '' (no. 357–13; compare Matt. 7:12; 25:40). This focus upon the Golden Rule and the solidarity, the cosmic interconnectedness, of God with the whole of his creation as central to the teaching—and life—of Jesus is found frequently in the Cayce readings.

The Cayce readings have not a little to say regarding the methodology of prayer and meditation—always given so as to be understood in a manner free of legalism or coercion of any kind, inner or outer. Generally the advice is simple. ''Enter into the holy of holies with thy God'' (no. 1376–1). This is a call to interiority, to meet with our Maker in the inner self, which is for the readings not only the primary arena of encounter with the living God, but ''the holy of holies,'' the self within the body (compare Matt. 6:6). And the human body, as we have seen to be true also of the faith-understanding of the Apostle Paul, is frequently described in the readings as the temple of God, or the temple of the Holy Spirit (compare 1 Cor. 3:16–17; 6:15, 19; 2 Cor. 6:16).

The earthly prayer life of Jesus continues, but now with unrestricted cosmic ranges of contact and effects. ''He makes intercession for man. They that call upon Him shall not be left empty-handed'' (no. 3213–1; see also no. 938–1; compare Rom. 8:34; Heb. 7:25). ''And His promise *is*, has been (for He changeth not), 'Though ye may be afar off, if ye call, I will hear—and answer speedily' " (no. 2524–3; see also no. 3902–2 and no. 2900–2; compare Acts 2:39; Luke 18:8; Jer. 33: 3).

With references again to the reciprocal aspect of the divine-human relationship, we note the perhaps surprising— "surprising" because the theme is found in almost no historic theological statements or creeds of the Christian church—affirmation that "He, thy God, thy Christ, is conscious of and hath need of thee" (no. 5064–1). Elsewhere we read a similar faith-claim, "First be conscious of this, that the Lord hath need of thee with thy faults, with thy virtues" (no. 3685–1).

This thesis of divine "need," of course, is not intended to suggest limitations upon the power of God. It means rather to remind us that the original purpose in the creation of souls was God's desire for companionship and that his will for us all is that we become not only companions but also coworkers, cocreators with him in the whole of his program for the universe (no. 1567–2). The following passage puts this grand theme in language as beautiful as it is touching,

How beautiful the face of those whom the Lord, the Christ smiles upon! He would walk and talk with thee, my children, if ye will but put away from thy mind those things and conditions that ye feel are in the way. For they are as naught compared to the great love that He has bestowed upon His brethren.

How beautiful the face, how lovely the clouds! In His presence abide; ye, *every one* of you, are before Him just now. His face is turned toward thee, His heart and hand is offered you. Will ye not accept Him just now? How glorious the knowledge of His presence should awaken in the hearts of you, for He is *lonely* without thee, for He has called each of you by name. Will ye fail Him now? (no. 254–76; compare 1 John 3:1; Rom. 10:15; 1:6; 1 Cor. 1:2)

A CONCLUDING WORD

In truth, anything that may be said after the last excerpt from the Cayce readings could be considered but an appendage or afterthought. A few words, however, may be in order to put the above themes in proper perspective. That is, we have been told that our God, and his Christ, have need of us for companionship and cooperation, to "be a witness for [our] Maker" in the specific "material activities in which [we] might enter into" (no. 5064–1). This call, as we have noted, is in fact an appeal to participate in the larger work of God in the world—and in the cosmos—even in his vast program and activity of universal redemption, reconciliation, restoration, and on-going creativity.

In the Cayce readings, however, our perception of and actual participation within a program of such grand cosmic scope do not necessarily imply what our society in common parlance calls some "big deal." When we are told to "be a channel of blessing to others [for this] is that purpose for which each soul has come into conscious activity in a material world," we are further informed that such activity may not be received with "thunderous applause" (no. 3161–1). This reading gives several of the specifics involved in what being "a channel of blessing to others" entails, a walk often modest in the worldly sense but never alone.

Self in the physical grows weary, because you are only human, because you are finite. You have a beginning, you have an end of your patience, your love, your hope, your fear, your desire. These are to be considered also—not as unto self, but when these problems arise know, as He has given, you cannot walk the whole way alone, but He has promised in the Christ Consciousness to give you strength, to give you life and that more abundant [compare John 10:10]. What then is life?—God, in power, in might, in the awareness of the strength needed to meet every problem day by day [compare Phil. 4:13; Col. 1:11].

Know it is in the little things, not by thunderous applause, not by the ringing of bells, nor the blowing of whistles, that the Son of man comes—humble, gently, kind, meek, lowly—for ''he that is the greatest among you serveth all'' [compare Isa. 28:10, 13; Matt. 11:29–30; Mark 9:35 and parallels]. (no. 3161–1)

We are told that ''He [the risen Christ] will come again and again in the hearts, in the minds, in the experiences of those that *love* His coming'' (no. 1152–1; compare 2 Pet. 3: 12). Christ Jesus ''offers His hand to those who are disturbed in any way, in any manner, in any problem, and He promises to give that peace—not as the world knows peace, but that peace of assurity that you are one with Him'' (no. 3165–1; compare John 14:27; 17:21).

EPILOGUE

THE EDGAR CAYCE readings repeatedly affirm that Jesus the Christ, in the Holy Spirit, continues to be present and at work in the world, especially with and within those who will let him and invite him. There is an abundance of materials available—also about the activities of Jesus' disciples after his resurrection and ascension and after the experience of the coming of the Holy Spirit with power on the festival of Pentecost (compare Acts 2:1–42).

There seems also to be discernible in the Cayce readings a special concern of Jesus for his church, even though his presence and work are not confined to its institutional expressions or organizations. Indeed, one definition of the church is that he [Jesus] who "was set as the Head of the church is the church" (no. 262–87; compare Matt. 16:13–20). The same reading goes on to specify that Jesus' role is central in the life of the church, that its "membership" consists of those who are in relationship with him as the Head of the church, accepting him as Mediator between God and oneself, between one's self and other selves. "An *individual* soul becomes aware that it has taken that Head, that Son, that Man even, to be the intermediator. That [association of such individuals in communion with the Head and thereby with one another] is the church. That is what is spoken of as the Holy Church" (no. 262–87; compare 1 Cor. 11:3; Eph.

5:23; Col. 1:18; 1 Tim. 2:5; Heb. 9:15; 12:24).

Elsewhere we read, "The true church is within you, as the Master, as the Christ gave . . . 'I to *you* am the bridegroom—I to *you* am the church. The kingdom is within *you*' " (no. 452–7; compare Luke 17:20–21; Mark 2:19–20; John 3:29). The Cayce readings, therefore, refuse to give any *ultimate* spiritual significance or authority to ecclesiastical organizations, structures, or personages, but they did advise several persons that it is well and wise to participate in such. "A particular church organization is well, for it centers the mind" (no. 3350–1). "As to the organization, choose that—not as a convenience for thee but where ye may serve the better, whatever its name" (no. 3342–1). "Render unto the church that which is the church, whether in creed or in organization, but render unto God, and Christ, the *service* that is His in whatever field of activity thou goest" (no. 556–1; compare Mark 12:13–17 and parallels).

As He has given, it will ever be found that Truth—whether in this or that schism or ism or cult—is of the one Source. Are there not trees of oak, of ash, of pine? There are the needs of these for meeting this or that experience. Hast thou chosen any one of these to be the *all* in thine usages in thine own life? Then, all will fill their place. Find not fault with *any*, but rather show forth as to just how good a pine, or ash, or oak, or *vine* thou art. (no. 254–87; compare John 15:1–11)

SELECTED BIBLIOGRAPHY

Adriance, Robert A. "The Journey." In *Journey to Mount Carmel*, edited by Violet M. Shelley. Virginia Beach, VA: A.R.E. Press, 1972.

Albright, W. F., & Mann, C. S. "Matthew." *The Anchor Bible*. Garden City, NY: Doubleday, 1973.

Anguttara-Nikaya. *The Book of Gradual Sayings*. Translated by F. L. Woodward. London: Luzac, 1951.

Betz, Otto. *What Do We Know About Jesus*. London: S.C.M. Press, 1968.

Bornkamm, Günther. *Jesus of Nazareth*. San Francisco: Harper & Row, 1975.

Bright, John. *A History of Israel*. Philadelphia: Westminster Press, 1959.

Bro, Harmon H. *Edgar Cayce on Religion and Psychic Experience*. New York: Paperback Library, 1970.

———"Finding the Way to Full Emptiness." *Venture Inward* 3, No. 1 (January-February 1987).

Brown, Raymond E. *"The Gospel According to John." The Anchor Bible*. New York: Doubleday, 1966.

Bruns, J. Edgar. *The Christian Buddhism of St. John*. New York: Paulist Press, 1971.

Cayce, Edgar Evans, and Cayce, Hugh Lynn. *The Outer Limits of Edgar Cayce's Power*. New York: Harper & Brothers, 1970.

Cayce, Hugh Lynn. *Venture Inward*. New York: Paperback Library, 1969.

Chadwick, Henry. *Early Christian Thought and the Classical Tradition*. Oxford: Oxford University Press, 1966.

Chambers, Franklin. *Juliana of Norwich*. New York: Harper & Brothers, 1955.

Chandogya Upanishad.

Cross, F. L. *The Early Christian Fathers*. London: Gerald Duckworth, 1960.

Davies, W. D. *Paul and Rabbinic Judaism*. London: S.P.C.K., 1955.

Dement, William C. *Some Must Watch, While Some Must Sleep*. San Francisco: W. H. Freeman, 1974.

Didache (Apostolic Fathers). Translated & edited by Kirsopp Lake. Cambridge: Harvard University Press, 1945.

Dowling, Levi H. *The Aquarian Gospel of Jesus the Christ*. Santa Monica, CA: De Vorss, 1969.

Drummond, Richard H. *Gautama the Buddha: An Essay in Religious Understanding*. Grand Rapids, MI: Eerdmans Publishing Co., 1974.

Easton, Stewart C. *Rudolf Steiner, Herald of a New Epoch*. Spring Valley, NY: The Anthroposophic Press, 1980.

Emmerich, Anne Catherine. *The Dolorous Passion of Our Lord Jesus Christ*. London: Burns & Oates, 1956.

Endo, Shusaku. *A Life of Jesus*. New York: Paulist Press, 1978.

Epiphanius. *Adversus Haereses*.

The Gospel of the Nativity of Mary.

Guillaume, Alfred. *Prophecy and Divination*. New York: Harper & Brothers, 1938.

Haraldsson, Erlendur. *Modern Miracles*. New York: Ballantine Books, 1987.

Hemleben, Johannes. *Rudolf Steiner*. East Grinstead, Sussex, U.K.: Henry Goulden, Ltd., 1975.

Hippolytus. *Ante-Nicene Fathers*.

Homilies. Clementine.

James, M. R. *The Apocryphal New Testament*. Oxford: The Clarendon Press, 1924.

Jerome. "Letters." *Epistula ad Demetriadem*.

Josephus, Flavius. *Against Apion*.

———. *History of the Jewish War*.

———. *Jewish Antiquities*.

Jung, C. J. *Memories, Dreams, Reflections*. Edited by Aniela Jaffé. New York: Random House, 1963.

Kittler, Glenn D. *Edgar Cayce on the Dead Sea Scrolls*. New York: Paperback Library, 1970.

Origen. *Commentarius in Ioannem*.

———. *Contra Celsum*.

———. *De Principiis*.

Pagels, Elaine. *The Gnostic Gospels*. New York: Random House, 1979.

The Protoevangelium of James.

Raymond of Capua, Blessed. *The Life of St. Catherine of Siena*. Translated by George Lamb. New York: P. J. Kennedy, 1960.

Rig-Veda.

Schillebeeckx, Edward. *Jesus, an Experiment in Christology*. New York: Crossroad, 1979.

Search for God. Virginia Beach, VA: A.R.E. Press, 1970.

Shakespeare, William. *Hamlet*.

Sheldon, Charles Monroe. *In His Steps*. New York: Grosset & Dunlap, 1935.

Skinner, John. *Prophecy and Religion*. Cambridge, England: The University Press, 1922.

Steiner, Johannes. *Therese Neumann*. Staten Island, NY: Alba House, 1967.

Steiner, Rudolf. *Background to the Gospel of St. Mark*. London: Rudolf Steiner Press, 1968.

——. *From Jesus to Christ*. London: Rudolf Steiner Press, 1973.

——. *The Fifth Gospel*. London: Rudolf Steiner Press, 1968.

——. *The Gospel of St. Luke*. London: Rudolf Steiner Press, 1975.

Streeter, B. H., and Appasamy, A. J. *The Message of Sadhu Sundar Singh*. New York: Macmillan, 1921.

Traherne, Thomas. *Centuries*. New York: Harper & Brothers, 1960.

Watson, Lyall. *Beyond Supernature*. New York: Bantam Books, 1988.

Weisheipl, James A., O.P. *Friar Thomas D'Aquino, His Life, Thought and Work*. Garden City, NY: Doubleday, 1974.

Zenger, Erich. "Jahwe und die Götter." *Theologie und Philosophie*. 1968.

INDEX

ABOUT THE AUTHOR

Richard Henry Drummond, Ph.D., has studied classics at the University of California, Los Angeles, and the University of Wisconsin, and was ordained as a Presbyterian minister in 1947. Since then, he has served as a field and educational missionary and also correspondent for *The Christian Century* magazine in Japan and taught classics and religious studies at a number of universities and seminaries there and in the United States.

Dr. Drummond is currently professor emeritus at University of Dubuque Theological Seminary and has lectured as a visiting professor at Aquinas Institute of Theology, Divine Word College, International Christian University (Japan), Luther Theological Seminary, Meiji Gakuin University (Tokyo), Old Dominion University, Tokyo Union Theological Seminary, Wartburg Theological Seminary, and Atlantic University.

EDGAR CAYCE'S WISDOM FOR THE NEW AGE

More information from the Edgar Cayce readings is available to you on hundreds of topics from astrology and arthritis to universal laws and world affairs, because Cayce's friends established an organization, the Association for Research and Enlightenment (A.R.E.), to facilitate his readings and make the information available for research.

Today over one hundred thousand members of the A.R.E. receive the bimonthly magazine *Venture Inward*, which contains articles on dream interpretation, past lives, health and diet tips, psychic archaeology, and psi research, as well as book reviews and interviews with leaders and authors in the metaphysical field. Members also receive extracts of medical and nonmedical readings and may do their own research in all of the over fourteen thousand readings that Edgar Cayce gave during his lifetime.

To receive more information about the association that continues to research and make available information on subjects in the Edgar Cayce readings, please write A.R.E., Dept. M, 67th and Atlantic Ave., Box 595, Virginia Beach, VA 23451-0595, or call (800) 333-4499. The A.R.E. will be happy to send you a packet of materials describing its current activities.

MIND MEETS BODY...
HEALTH MEETS HAPPINESS...
SPIRIT MEETS SERENITY...

In his writings, spiritual advisor Edgar Cayce counseled thousands with his extraordinary, yet practical guidance to the mind/body/spirit connection. Now, the Edgar Cayce series, based on actual readings by the renowned psychic, can provide you with insights in the search for understanding and meaning in life.

KEYS TO HEALTH: The Promise and Challenge of Holism
Eric A. Mein, M.D.
_____ 95616-9 $4.99 U.S./$5.99 CAN.

REINCARNATION: Claiming Your Past, Creating Your Future
Lynn Elwell Sparrow
_____ 95754-8 $4.99 U.S./$5.99 CAN.

DREAMS: Tonight's Answers for Tomorrow's Questions
Mark Thurston, Ph.D.
_____ 95771-8 $5.50 U.S./$6.50 CAN.

AWAKENING YOUR PSYCHIC POWERS
Henry Reed
_____ 95868-4 $5.99 U.S./$6.99 CAN.

HEALING MIRACLES: Using Your Body Energies for Spiritual and Physical Health
William A. McGarey, M.D.
_____ 95948-6 $5.99 U.S./$6.99 CAN.

Publishers Book and Audio Mailing Service
P.O. Box 120159, Staten Island, NY 10312-0004
Please send me the book(s) I have checked above. I am enclosing $_____ (please add $1.50 for the first book, and .50 for each additional book to cover postage and handling. Send check or money order only—no CODs) or charge my VISA, MASTERCARD, DISCOVER or AMERICAN EXPRESS card.

Card Number_____

Expiration date_____Signature_____

Name_____

Address_____

City_____State/Zip _____
Please allow six weeks for delivery. Prices subject to change without notice. Payment in U.S. funds only. New York residents add applicable sales tax.   CAYCE 12/96